Susanne Mueller (Hg./Ed.)

MODERNES KASACHSTAN
MODERN KAZAKHSTAN

Beiträge deutscher Investoren
Contributions of German Investors

The Economy & Culture Series
Books from Investors for Investors, by Managers for Managers

The Economy & Culture Series presents books on the achievements of foreign investors in different countries along with their experiences in business, corporate culture and leadership. It is issued by Cross-Culture Publishing, Dr. Susanne Mueller, Frankfurt/Main and designed as a medium for Corporate Communication. All the volumes in this series are available on the international book market including Amazon. They convey information and provide orientation for entrepreneurs, companies, organisations, institutions and executives who intend to expand or invest within and outside of the European Union.

Cross-Culture Publishing is a publishing house specializing in publications about the relationship between economy and culture. It emphasizes the fact that doing business abroad requires more than professional expertise and knowledge about the legal conditions for investment in a foreign country.

Besides providing information on the economic parameters and legal information, each book in *The Economy & Culture Series* imparts knowledge on the norms and values of social and business life in a particular country and presents it all within the framework of history, present society and the economy. It delivers information for business people in general and investors in particular by advising on the business culture and management style in that country.

In short, the set of volumes in *The Economy & Culture Series* focuses on the human dimension of cross-cultural business cooperation. It essentially serves as a basis for synergetic economic cooperation and to develop a mutual understanding between culturally diverse partners.

Vol. 1	Management Guide LITAUEN	ISBN 3-939044-04-0
Vol. 2	Management Guide LETTLAND	ISBN 3-939044-01-6
Vol. 3	Management Guide ESTLAND	ISBN 3-939044-02-4
Vol. 4	Management Guide POLEN	ISBN 3-939044-03-2
Vol. 5	Management Guide PORTUGAL	ISBN 3-939044-04-0
Vol. 6	Management Guide TÜRKEI	ISBN 978-3-939044-07-09
Vol. 7	Management Guide TURKEY	ISBN 978-3-939044-08-6
Vol. 8	Management Guide RUMÄNIEN	ISBN 978-3-939044-10-9
Vol. 9	Management Guide ROMANIA	ISBN 978-3-939044-12-3
Vol.10	Management Guide BULGARIA	ISBN 978-3-939044-11-6
Vol.11	MODERN SOUTHEAST EUROPE	ISBN 978-3-939044-15-4
Vol.12	MODERN TURKEY	ISBN 978-3-939044-14-7
Vol.13	Management Guide NEW ANDORRA	ISBN 978-3-939044-13-0
Vol.14	MODERNES SPANIEN	ISBN 978-3-939044-05-5
Vol.15	MODERNES BRASILIEN	ISBN 978-3-939044-16-1
Vol.16	MODERNES PANAMA	ISBN 978-3-939044-24-6
Vol. 17	MODERNES KOLUMBIEN	ISBN 978-3-939044-23-9
Vol. 18	MODERNES PERU	ISBN 978-3-939044-26-0
Vol. 19	MODERNES CHILE	ISBN 978-3-939044-27-7
Vol. 20	MODERNES MALAYSIA	ISBN978-3-939044-36-9
Vol. 21	MODERNES KASACHSTAN	ISBN 978-3-939044-47-5

Subscriptions to: mail@cc-publishing.com
Cross-Culture Publishing, Dr. Susanne Mueller
Bettinastrasse 30, D-60325 Frankfurt/M., Germany
www.cc-publishing.com

Susanne Mueller (Hg./Ed.)

MODERNES KASACHSTAN
MODERN KAZAKHSTAN

Beiträge deutscher Investoren
Contributions of German Investors

Cross-Culture Publishing
Frankfurt am Main 2018

Bibliographic information published by the Deutsche Nationalbibliothek.
The Deutsche Nationalbibliothek lists this publication in the Deutsche Nationalbibliografie;
detailed bibliographic data are available in the Internet at
http://dnb.d-nb.de
ISBN 978-3-939044-47-5

First Edition – 2018
Published by Cross-Culture Publishing, Frankfurt/Main
Editorial Assistance: Nelly Thomas, Effective in English, Langenselbold, www.nellythomas.de
Editing and Layout by Dr. Susanne Mueller and Marius P. Weber
Cover designed by Marius P. Weber, Bucharest
Printed by Graspo CZ, a.s., Pod Šternberkem 324, 763 02 Zlín • http://www.graspo.com

Copyright © 2018 by Cross-Culture Publishing, Dr Susanne Mueller
Frankfurt/Main, Germany
All rights reserved. No part of the book may be translated or reproduced in any form, by photostat, microform, retrieval system, or any means, without the prior written permission of the publisher.

www.cc-publishing.com

Liability Disclaimer: The editor and publisher are not liable or responsible for the accuracy or completeness of any information provided in this book. We assume no liability or responsibility for any damages arising from a reader's use of, or inability to use, this book. By accessing the information in this book, you agree that the editor and publisher shall not be liable to you for any loss or injury caused in procuring, compiling, or delivering the information. In no event will the editor, publisher or the contributors of information to this book be liable to you or anyone else for any action taken by you in reliance on such information or for any consequential, special, or similar damages.
The editor and publisher are not responsible for anything whatsoever on internet sites that the book links to or provides links to. The use of links is solely at the discretion of users and any damage resulting from the use of a link is entirely the responsibility of the user.

Inhalt

Vorwort des Verlages   9

Teil 1. Kasachstan heute   11

Wirklich große Veränderungen der Wirtschaftsstruktur sind in Kasachstan geplant. *Interview mit Prof. Dr. Wilhelm Bender, Former Chairman of the Executive Board Fraport AG, Independent Director and Member of the Board of Directors bei Sovereign Wealth Fund Samruk-Kazyna Joint Stock Company, Kasachstan*   13

Deutsche Unternehmen als Investoren in Kasachstan sehr gefragt. *Von Peter Tils, Co-Chairman des Deutsch-Kasachischen Wirtschaftsrates*   17

Teil 2. Modernes Kasachstan – attraktives Investmentziel   21

EAWU und Neue Seidenstraße bieten langfristige, hervorragende Marktchancen und machen Kasachstan zu einem idealen Standort für deutsche Unternehmen. *Interview mit Herrn Dr. Robert Breitner, Delegierter der Deutschen Wirtschaft für Zentralasien mit Sitz in Almaty*   23

Hervorragende Chancen für Investoren in Kasachstan. *Von Hans-Joachim Bischoff, INVEST KAZAKH Representative Germany*   27

Rechtliche Grundlagen für Geschäfte mit kasachischen Partnern. *Von Prof. Dr. Hans-Joachim Schramm und Dimitri Olejnik, Ostinstitut Wismar*   36

Teil 3. Deutsche Firmen formen das moderne Kasachstan mit   41

BASF in Zentralasien   43

BASF: Kundennähe und Entwicklung lokaler Talente. *Interview mit Frau Saule Baitzhaunova, Managing Director, BASF Central Asia LLP*   45

Green Energy 3000 Gruppe projektiert ein 63 MWp Solarkraftwerk in Südkasachstan	49
Kasachstan bietet für Erneuerbare Energien äußerst attraktive Rahmenbedingungen. *Interview mit Herrn Dipl.-Ing. Andreas Renker, Geschäftsführer, Green Energy 3000 Holding GmbH, Leipzig*	51
LORENZ Handels GmbH, Neuhof, Germany und Managing Company Shanyrak Ltd., Astana, Kasachstan	55
Erfolg in Kasachstan. Die Lorenz-Strategie: Klein beginnen, aktiv sein und korrekt arbeiten, mit ersten Erfolgen Vertrauen aufbauen und dann wachsen. *Interview mit Herrn Alexander Lorenz, General Manager der Managing Company Shanyrak GmbH, Astana*	57
Amazonen-Werke H. Dreyer GmbH & Co.KG	61
Amazone: Agronomische und technische Lösungen für nachhaltigen Pflanzenbau in den eurasischen Steppen. *Interview mit Herrn Dr. rer. nat. Tobias Meinel, General Director, TOO Amazone, Astana, Kasachstan*	63
Anlage für Rohrisolierung Isoplus Central Asia LLP	67
Erst wenn wir die lokale Mentalität verstanden haben und genug Geduld mitbringen, können wir erfolgreich sein. *Interview mit Herrn Leonard Stein, General Manager, Isoplus Central Asia LLP*	69
Teil 4. Modernes Kasachstan im Bild	**73**
Annexe	157

Contents

Preface by the Publisher   10

Part 1. Kazakhstan Today   **99**

Exceptionally great changes planned for the economic structure
in Kazakhstan. *Interview with Prof. Dr. Wilhelm Bender, former
Chairman, Executive Board, Fraport AG, Independent Director
and Member of the Board of Directors of Sovereign Wealth Fund
Samruk-Kazyna Joint Stock Company, Kazakhstan*   101

German companies in high demand as investors in Kazakhstan.
By Peter Tils, Co-Chairman of the German-Kazakh Business Council   105

**Part 2. Modern Kazakhstan – Attractive Destination for
Foreign Investment**   **109**

The EAEU and the New Silk Road offer excellent long-term
market opportunities and make Kazakhstan an ideal site
for German companies. *Interview with Dr. Robert Breitner,
Representative of German Economic Affairs for Central Asia with
headquarters in Almaty*   109

Kazakhstan offers excellent opportunities for investors. *By
Hans-Joachim Bischoff, Representative Germany, KAZAKH INVEST*   115

The legal basis for business with Kazakh partners. *By Prof. Dr.
Hans-Joachim Schramm and Dimitri Olejnik, Ostinstitut Wismar,
Germany*   123

Part 3. German Companies Help Shape Modern Kazakhstan   **127**

BASF Central Asia LLP   129

BASF: proximity and local empowerment. *Interview with Ms.
Saule Baitzhaunova, Managing Director, BASF Central Asia LLP*   131

Green Energy 3000 Group plans a 63 MWp solar power plant in southern Kazakhstan	135
Kazakhstan offers extremely attractive conditions for Renewable Energy. *Interview with Mr. Andreas Renker, Dipl.-Ing, Managing Director Green Energy 3000 Holding GmbH, Leipzig*	137
Europe-Asia Bridge: LORENZ Handels GmbH, Neuhof, Germany and Managing Company Shanyrak Ltd., Astana, Kasakhstan	141
Success in Kazakhstan. The Lorenz strategy: Start small, stay active and work right. Based on initial success, build trust and then grow. *Interview with Mr. Alexander Lorenz, General Manager of the Managing Company Shanyrak Ltd, Astana*	143
Amazonen-Werke H. Dreyer GmbH & Co.KG	147
Amazone: Agronomic and technical solutions for sustainable crop production in the Eurasian Steppe. *Interview with Dr. rer. nat. Tobias Meinel, General Director of TOO Amazone, Astana, Kazakhstan*	148
Plant for high-performance pipe insulation Isoplus Central Asia LLP	152
We can only succeed once we have understood the local mentality and been patient enough. *Interview with Mr. Leonard Stein, General Manager, Isoplus Central Asia LLP*	154

Part 4. Modern Kazakhstan in Pictures — 73

Annexe — 157

Vorwort des Verlages

MODERNES KASACHSTAN – wenig Vorstellung hat man zurzeit noch in Deutschland von dieser in Zentralasien gelegenen jungen Republik, obwohl einige hundert deutsche Firmen bereits kurz nach ihrer Gründung im Jahre 1991 dem Ruf des Präsidenten folgten, die Entwicklung des Landes mit ihrem Know-how zu unterstützen. Sehr gern macht Cross-Culture Publishing daher das Land weiteren deutschen Firmen als künftigen Investoren bekannt. Unser Verlag versteht sich prinzipiell als „Brückenbauer". Dies ist die erste Publikation, die Kasachstan aus der Sicht deutscher Firmen vorstellt.

Es wird viele überraschen zu erfahren, dass Kasachstan siebenmal größer als Deutschland und seine Hauptstadt Astana wahrscheinlich die jüngste der Welt ist. Im Juli 2018 feierte sie ihr 20-jähriges Bestehen mit dem Slogan „Astana – Hauptstadt der großen Steppe". Die moderne Millionenstadt, Location der Expo 2017, erinnert stolz an ihre Wurzeln: Sie erwuchs innerhalb von historisch kürzester Zeit aus der großen asiatischen Steppe heraus, die ca. ein Drittel der Landesfläche einnimmt und unter ihrer Oberfläche reich an Bodenschätzen ist. Viele Motive künstlerischer Stadtdekoration zeugen vom früheren Nomadenleben der Kasachen in der Steppe, zum Beispiel die Jurte, das Kamel, das Pferd, der Falkner, der Bogenschütze, das Beige-Braun des Steppengrases. Man findet sie übrigens auch in anderen Städten. Alle wachsen, überall entstehen großzügige neue Stadtteile. Kasachstan verfügt über viel Raum und die Bevölkerung des Landes ist jung, optimistisch und mehrsprachig: Kasachisch, Russisch und Englisch generell. Auch Deutschsprachige gibt es im ganzen Land; dafür sorgen Deutschkurse in über 20 Kulturzentren der Organisation der Kasachstan-Deutschen *Wiedergeburt,* komplementiert durch Deutschunterricht in einigen Schulen der großen Städte. Geheiratet wird zeitig, vier bis fünf Kinder in den Familien sind die Regel – und ein bis zwei Autos auch, das wichtigste Mobilitätsmittel des Landes.

Die Entwicklung städtischer wie ländlicher Infrastruktur, wie zum Beispiel Schnellbahnen, gehört zu den großen Aufgaben und Zielen der Regierung und bietet deutschen Investoren bedeutende Chancen. Sie bestehen auch in den Wirtschaftssektoren Bergbau und Erneuerbare Energien, für die große unerschlossene Potenzen in den Steppengebieten liegen. Kasachstan ist bereits heute die am schnellsten wachsende Volkswirtschaft Zentralasiens und in 2050 will das Land zu den 30 am meisten entwickelten Industrieländern der Welt gehören.

Innovative Investoren sind hoch willkommen!

Frankfurt/M., August 2018   *Dr. Susanne Mueller*
                                                                Cross-Culture Publishing

Preface by the Publisher

MODERN KAZAKHSTAN: Currently, not everyone in Germany may have an idea of this young republic located in Central Asia. Established in 1991, several hundred German companies quickly followed its president's invitation to support Kazakhstan's development with their know-how. It is a pleasure for Cross-Culture Publishing to introduce the country to additional German companies as future investors. Our publishing house sees itself as "bridge builder" in principle. This is the first publication to present Kazakhstan from the viewpoint of German firms.

Many readers will be surprised to learn that Kazakhstan is seven times larger than Germany, while its capital, Astana, is probably the youngest in the world. The city celebrated its 20th anniversary in July 2018 under the slogan: "Astana: capital of the Great Steppe". With a population of over one million and site of the Expo 2017, the modern capital proudly reminds us of its roots: Astana grew out of the great Eurasian Steppe within a historically short time. The Kazakh Steppe occupies a third of the nation's territory and below its surface, it is rich in mineral resources. The many artistic themes found in Astana bear witness to earlier Kazakh nomad life in the Steppe, for example: the yurt tent dwelling, camel, horse, falconer, archer and the beige-brown of the grasslands. These are also present in the other cities. New spacious urban districts are developing everywhere. There is plenty of space in Kazakhstan and the country's population is young, optimistic and multilingual: Kazakh, Russian and English in general. In addition, German-speakers are found all across the country thanks to German courses held in approx. twenty cultural centers of the Kazakh-German organization *Wiedergeburt* [Revival], complemented by German lessons in several large city schools. Weddings take place early in life and four to five children per family are the rule. Each family also has one or two automobiles: the most important means of transportation in the country.

The development of urban and rural infrastructures, such as high-speed railways, is just one of the great tasks and goals by the government and offers significant opportunities to German investors. Opportunities also exist in the mining and Renewable Energy economic sectors where there is a huge untapped potential in the Steppe areas. Kazakhstan already has the strongest growing economy in Central Asia today and by 2050, the nation will belong to the thirty most developed industrial countries in the world.

Innovative investors are highly welcome!

Frankfurt/M., August 2018   *Dr. Susanne Mueller*
                                                             Cross-Culture Publishing

Teil 1

Kasachstan heute

Wirklich große Veränderungen der Wirtschaftsstruktur sind in Kasachstan geplant

Interview mit Prof. Dr. Wilhelm Bender, Former Chairman of the Executive Board Fraport AG, Independent Director and Member of the Board of Directors bei Sovereign Wealth Fund Samruk-Kazyna Joint Stock Company, Kasachstan

CCP: *Herr Professor Bender, Sie haben sehr viele Verpflichtungen, daher zuerst vielen Dank für Ihre Bereitschaft zu diesem Interview für MODERNES KASACHSTAN. Sie kennen das Land gut. Nennen Sie doch bitte spontan einige Charakteristika des modernen Kasachstan, so wie Sie es erlebt haben bei Ihren Reisen.*

PWB: Ich kannte Kasachstan überhaupt nicht. Ich habe erst einmal gelernt, wie riesig das Land ist. Die Größe schafft natürlich entsprechende Herausforderungen an Versorgung der Bevölkerung, Infrastruktur, Mobilität etc., Herausforderungen, die die Regierung und die nationalen Unternehmen meistern müssen.

Auch unter diesem Aspekt ist das, was sich das Land an Wachstum und Modernisierung vorgenommen hat, besonders beeindruckend.

CCP: *Ja, das ist wirklich sehr beeindruckend und die Regierung hat große Pläne für die Weiterentwicklung. Daher ruft sie erfahrene ausländische Experten wie Sie ins Land. Warum eigentlich, bestimmt gibt es auch im eigenen Land Experten mit viel Auslandserfahrung.*

PWB: Regierung und Staatsfonds suchen den externen Sachverstand aus gutem Grund. Sie wollen unsere Erfahrungen zum Beispiel bei Börsengängen nutzen und mit hohem Zeitdruck die Unternehmen und darüber sicher das Land verändern.

CCP: *Versteht sich. Lassen Sie uns bitte ein wenig Einblick nehmen in Ihre Erfahrung, Herr Professor.*

PWB: Ich war 17 Jahre CEO bei Fraport in Frankfurt, mit Börsengang in 2001 und vorher CEO bei der Spedition Schenker. Ich habe auch breite AR-Erfahrung, zum Beispiel bei ThyssenKrupp Services, Adtranz, Bombardier, Techem, Signal Iduna, LH Cargo, MTU und anderen Unternehmen. Schließlich habe ich auch ehrenamtliche Erfahrung in der Wirtschaftsförderung.

CCP: *Das ist ein sehr überzeugendes Profil, Herr Professor. Nun wurden Sie von der kasachischen Regierung um Unterstützung gebeten bei der Modernisierung des Landes. Welche Veränderungen sind dort geplant?*

PWB: Große, wirklich große Veränderungen der Wirtschaftsstruktur sind geplant. Also zum Beispiel Privatisierungen über Verkäufe, Teilverkäufe und IPO. Außerdem sollen international bewährte und akzeptierte Standards in der Unternehmensführung, in der Struktur der Gesellschaften und ihrer Organe beschlossen und durchgesetzt werden, das bedeutet Governance- und Compliance-Regeln.

CCP: *Das ist ein erfreuliches Ziel, jedoch sicherlich nicht leicht zu realisieren. Was ist vor allen Dingen notwendig zu erreichen?*

PWB: Die Staatsquote bei den Unternehmen muss drastisch gesenkt werden. Der Staat will sich ganz oder teilweise aus Schlüsselunternehmen zurückziehen. Das geht nicht auf Knopfdruck. Das wissen wir von Strukturveränderungen auch bei uns. Die Non-Executive und Independent Directors – also zum Beispiel ich – werden durch die Mitgliedschaft im Board eng in das unternehmerische Geschehen einbezogen.

CCP: *Privatisierung ist ein bedeutender Vorgang, der auch vom Ausland stark beobachtet wird.*

PWB: Ganz richtig, das ist vielleicht sogar der bedeutendste Prozess für die Modernisierung, Dafür muss um Überzeugung nach innen gerungen werden: in der Gesellschaft, in den Unternehmen. Veränderungen generell, vor allem jedoch Privatisierungen müssen als Chance gesehen und mitgetragen und nicht als Bedrohung des eigenen Status verstanden werden. Das ist ein ganz schwieriger Kommunikationsprozess, jedoch notwendig. Sofern er gelingt, wird auch das Vertrauen von außen wachsen.

CCP: *Kasachstan benötigt ein neues Image, nicht wahr?*

PWB: Ja, und das ist nur durch interne Reformen erreichbar. Dadurch wird die Akzeptanz bei ausländischen Investoren erhöht, der internationale Kapitalmarkt und die Anleger wie die Politik werden überzeugt werden. Die Eröffnung des Internationalen Finanzzentrums ist dazu schon ein bedeutender Schritt.

CCP: *Könnten Sie nun bitte beschreiben, wie Sie konkret Einfluss nehmen auf wirtschaftliche Veränderungen?*

PWB: Anfang März hat mich Premierminister *Bakytzhan Sagintayev* gefragt, ob ich bereit bin, in den Board von *Samruk-Kazyna* einzutreten, das ist ein riesiger Staatsfonds. Ihm gehört die Post- und die Eisenbahn-Gesellschaft, der Öl- und Gas-Konzern KazMunay Gaz, die Uran-Gesellschaft, Air Astana, die Flughäfen und viele andere große Gesellschaften, praktisch alles, was für das Land, seine Infrastruktur und das Zusammenwirken der Wirtschaft wichtig ist. Die Marktkapitalisierung von *Samruk-Kazyna* beträgt über 100 Mrd. USD. Zum Vergleich: der Börsenwert der Deutschen Bank beträgt 22 Mrd., der Firma Daimler-Benz 78 Mrd. und der Lufthansa 12 Mrd. Euro.

CCP: *Das ist wirklich ein gewaltiger Wert. Und wie funktioniert dieser Fond?*

PWB: In Kasachstan gilt das One-Tier-System. Das heißt, der einheitliche *Board of Directors* besteht aus *Executive Members* und *Non-Executive Members*. Es gibt also nicht wie bei uns Vorstand und Aufsichtsrat. Es gilt das angelsächsische System. Für die *Non-Executive* und *Independent Directors*, also zum Beispiel für mich, bedeutet dies mehr Einfluss und mehr Einbezug in das unternehmerische Geschehen.

CCP: *Aus wie vielen Personen besteht dieses Board?*

PWB: Der Board von *Samruk-Kazyna* besteht aus dem Premierminister als Chairman, dem Finanzminister, dem Wirtschaftsminister, dem CEO des Funds und drei *Independent Directors*, einschließlich mir. Es wird also nicht „durchregiert". Der wichtigste Ausschuss des Boards, *das Audit Committee,* besteht nur aus den Independent Directors und alle drei sind Ausländer.

CCP: *Sie werden also wesentlich am Prozess der Privatisierung mitwirken.*

PWB: Ja, und Privatisierung nicht nur der Infrastrukturgesellschaften, das ist ein ganz wesentliches Ziel des Präsidenten und der Regierung. Das öffnet für westliche Investoren erhebliche Chancen: einerseits für Beteiligung an Unternehmen, andererseits eröffnen sich auch Chancen für Zulieferer. Wirtschaftliches Wachstum wird auch die Konsumfähigkeit der Kasachen stärken. Das Land braucht eine stabile Binnennachfrage.

CCP: *Präsident Nasarbajev hat das Ziel, Kasachstan bis 2050 zu den 30 am stärksten entwickelten Ländern der Erde zu führen. Was muss außer und nach Privatisierung noch geschehen, um dieses Ziel zu erreichen?*

PWB: Weitere notwendige Veränderungen sind der Aufbau zukunftsfähiger, wachstumsstarker Industrien, Verminderung der Abhängigkeit von Rohstoff-Industrien und Stärkung des Dienstleistungssektors. Curricula sind zu ändern genauso wie Mentalitäten.

CCP: *Träger der Zukunft ist die Jugend des Landes. Wie schätzen Sie die junge Generation in Kasachstan ein?*

PWB: Kasachstan ist ein Land im Aufbruch. Das gilt für die Führung, die wirtschaftliche Elite ebenso wie für die Menschen, die ich kennengelernt habe. Die jungen Leute sind hochmotiviert und sehr gut ausgebildet, oft im Ausland. Sie wissen, dass ihr Aufstieg von der eigenen Leistung abhängt.

Ich will gerne meinen Beitrag leisten zur Veränderung in Kasachstan, jedoch auch, um das Interesse deutscher Investoren an Kasachstan zu wecken.

CCP: *Vielen Dank, Herr Professor, für Ihre überzeugenden Statements. Sie haben eine große Aufgabe, die jedoch auch eine Chance ist, das moderne Kasachstan mit Ihren Erfahrungen mit zu formen. Wir wünschen Ihnen viel Erfolg.*

Prof. Dr. Wilhelm Bender
w.bender@frankfurt-airportoffice.de

Deutsche Unternehmen als Investoren in Kasachstan sehr gefragt

Von Peter Tils, Co-Chairman des Deutsch-Kasachischen Wirtschaftsrates

Kasachstan begann sehr früh, eng mit internationalen Partnern zu kooperieren. Bereits zu Beginn seines Transformationsprozesses in den frühen neunziger Jahren hat Kasachstan internationale Investoren eingeladen, seine Öl- und Gas-Ressourcen mit ausländischem Know-how zu entwickeln. Damit erlaubte das Land einen starken Wettbewerb für die lokale Ölindustrie und steigerte die Effizienz der Öl- und Gasgewinnung erheblich. Öl- und Gas-Unternehmen aus China, Frankreich, Großbritannien, Italien, Russland, USA und anderen Ländern sind daher seit Jahren in dem Land präsent. Präsident Nasarbajev gründete einen *Rat Ausländischer Investoren (Foreign Investors Council (FIC))*, der einen ständigen Dialog mit ausländischen Partnern ermöglichte und zu einer Vielzahl von investorenfreundlichen regulatorischen und politischen Entscheidungen führte. Dies war unter anderem die Grundlage für die teilweise bedeutenden zweistelligen Wachstumsraten der kasachischen Wirtschaft von Mitte der 90er Jahre bis zum Ausbruch der Finanzkrise 2007/8. Darüber hinaus schuf Kasachstan einen Öl-Reservefond, der in den Folgejahren der Finanz- und Ölkrise effektiv eingesetzt wurde, um die Auswirkungen auf die kasachische Wirtschaft abzumildern. Heute hat Kasachstan einen Bestand von über 300 Mrd. USD ausländischer Direktinvestitionen, ist zurück bei Wachstumsraten von ca. vier Prozent und blickt optimistisch nach vorn.

Nachdem Kasachstan sich zu Beginn auf seine umfangreichen natürlichen Ressourcen konzentriert hatte, fokussiert man sich nun auf die weitere Diversifikation der lokalen Wirtschaft. Hier wird auch der Finanzsektor einbezogen. Nachdem Astana Gastgeber der Expo 2017 war, entwickelt Kasachstan nun aufbauend auf der eindrucksvollen Expo-Infrastruktur sein neues *Astana International Financial Center (AIFC)*. Auch hier wieder bemüht sich Kasachstan um die Internationalisierung eines weiteren Wirtschaftszweiges.

Die positive Entwicklung wichtiger Nachbarländer, die Integration in regionale Organisationen wie die *Eurasische Wirtschaftsunion* und die *Zentralasiatische Kooperation* sollten Astana erlauben, sich in das regionale wie in das globale Finanzsystem einzubinden. Das AIFC arbeitet mit einem eigenen Rechtssystem, das auf englischem Recht basiert. Der Rechtsrahmen fokussiert auf Transparenz und Anlegerschutz. Steuerliche Sonderregelungen sollten eine positive Entwicklung des AIFC unterstützen. Die Zusammenarbeit mit dem *Shanghai Stock Exchange* und dem *American Stock Exchange NASDAQ* sollte internationale Erfahrung und Know-how einbringen. Das AIFC fokussiert insbesondere auf *Capital Markets, Asset Management, Financial Technologies, Islamic Finance* und *Private Banking*. Es ist das einzige Finanzzentrum dieser Art im *Commonwealth of Independent States (CIS)*. Die offizielle Eröffnung wurde im Rahmen einer neu gegründeten Konferenz, den *Astana Financial Days*, mit einer beeindruckenden Veranstaltung am 5. Juli 2018 gefeiert. Die Konferenz ermöglichte einen intensiven Dialog mit nationalen und internationalen Partnern über die Erwartungen an das neue AIFC sowie über internationale Trends in der Finanz- und regionalen Entwicklung. Die Konferenz und die offizielle Eröffnung unterstrichen die Ernsthaftigkeit der kasachischen Bemühungen, diesen neuen Eckpfeiler für eine solide und stabile wirtschaftliche Entwicklung des Landes und seiner Menschen zu einem Erfolg zu machen.

Ein offenes Thema ist die zur Zeit heftig diskutierte Frage, welche Vermögenswerte (Assets) in Astana gehandelt werden sollen, um die notwendige Liquidität für verschiedene Kapitalmarktinstrumente zu generieren. Schlüssel für den Erfolg wird die 3. Privatisierungsrunde sein, die von der Regierung angekündigt wurde. Man hört von ersten Unternehmen, die in dem neu gegründeten *Astana Stock Exchange* gelistet werden sollen, unter anderen *Kazatomprom, Air Astana* und *KazTelekom*. Wichtige kasachische Unternehmen wie *Kazmunaigaz* sollten folgen. Darüber hinaus könnten auch bestimmte Anleihen von Firmen oder der Regierung gelistet werden. Dies ist eine Voraussetzung für die Schaffung von Liquidität, die für einen attraktiven Finanzplatz benötigt wird, wo internationale Asset Manager, staatliche Reservefonds und Privatpersonen aktiv werden sollten. Bei der Eröffnung gab es Gerüchte darüber, dass sogar chinesische Namen gelistet werden könnten. Kommt all dies zusammen mit der Bereitschaft der aufstrebenden regionalen Partner zur Zusammenarbeit, besteht eine gute Chance für den Erfolg des neuen AIFC.

Deutschland und seine dynamische Wirtschaft standen schon immer im Blickpunkt der kasachischen Regierung. Deutsche Einwanderer spielten eine positive Rolle bei der Entwicklung des sowjetischen Kasachstan und vor allem Präsident Nasarbajev schätzt ihren positiven Einfluss auf die kasachische Wirtschaft. Nach der Wiedervereinigung Deutschlands verließen mehr als 700 000 Kasachstan-Deutsche das Land. Heute möchte Kasachstan deutsche Firmen gern überzeugen, im Land zu investieren. Da Deutschland aus historischen Gründen nicht stark in der Öl- und Gas-Industrie ist, erwartet Kasachstan, dass deutsche Unternehmen helfen, die kasachische Wirtschaft weiter zu diversifizieren. Die Entwicklungen im Jahr 2013 mit dem Preisverfall vor allem in der Ölindustrie führten zu erheblichen Bemühungen für eine verstärkte Diversifikation. Im Jahre 2010 wurde der *Deutsch-Kasachische Wirtschaftsrat (German-Kazakh Business Council)* gegründet, basierend auf einem *Memorandum of Understanding,* das während des Besuchs von Bundeskanzlerin Merkel in Astana unterzeichnet wurde. Gründungsmitglieder waren unter anderen Verbände wie der Ost-*Ausschuss der Deutschen Wirtschaft e. V., der Osteuropaverein der Deutschen Wirtschaft e. V.* (beide fusionierten inzwischen) sowie die *National Chamber of Entrepreneurs of the Republic of Kazakhstan „Atameken".* Der *Deutsch-Kasachische Wirtschaftsrat* wurde dann in 2012 durch das *Deutsch-Kasachische Rohstoffabkommen* ergänzt. Es sollte deutschen Unternehmen Zugriff auf Kasachstans reiche Ressourcen an Rohstoffen und Seltenen Erden sichern, und Kasachstan mit neuen Technologien aus Deutschland versorgen.

Der *Deutsch-Kasachische Wirtschaftsrat* hat sich bereits zehnmal getroffen. Sein Ziel, deutsche Investitionen nach Kasachstan zu erleichtern und Investitionsvorhaben durch die Unterstützung von kasachischer Seite zu fördern, wurde erfüllt. Der Rat hat zahlreiche Investitionsvorhaben diskutiert und dazu beigetragen, sie zu implementieren, war auch Plattform für die Ansprache von Investitionshürden und diente dem Austausch von Erfahrungen, die Unternehmen in Kasachstan und Deutschland gemacht hatten. Die Diskussionen sind konkret, oft mit erfolgreichen Follow-ups. Seit 2005 belaufen sich die deutschen Investitionen in Kasachstan auf inzwischen auf mehr als USD 3,5 Mrd., und viele neue Projekte sind in Vorbereitung. Es ist ein gutes Zeichen, dass viele Unternehmen Gewinne im Land reinvestieren.

In diesem Zusammenhang erwarten die Unternehmen, dass die Euler-Hermes Abdeckung, die die Bundesregierung für den Export gewährt, in der zweiten Hälfte von 2018 wieder aufgenommen wird. Deutschland hatte die Exportabdeckung in 2008 nach Turbulenzen im kasachischen Bankensektor gestoppt, und Verhandlungen zur Wiederherstellung dauern bis heute an. Für viele Unternehmen ist diese staatliche Unterstützung entscheidend, um bedeutende Investitionsprojekte zu realisieren, die durch beträchtliche Maschinen- und Technologieexporte unterstützt werden.

Kasachstan rangiert heute vergleichsweise hoch in verschiedenen globalen Kennzahlen und Rankings, zum Beispiel in Bezug auf Wettbewerbsfähigkeit, Regierungspolitik und Steuerklima, und liegt zurzeit auf Platz 29 von 130 Volkswirtschaften, was die Entwicklung des Humankapitals angeht. Von Anfang an investierte die Regierung substantiell in lokale Bildungseinrichtungen und förderte auch mit öffentlichen Mitteln Stipendien im Ausland. Mehr als 10 000 Studenten profitierten davon. Die meisten jüngeren Führungskräfte in Politik und Wirtschaft verfügen über eine ausländische Ausbildung und gute Sprachkenntnisse. Als eine der wichtigsten Herausforderungen für die Zukunft sieht Kasachstan auch die Digitalisierung der Wirtschaft an. In diesem Bereich werden lokale Initiativen, internationale Zusammenarbeit und Projekte entwickelt.

Kasachstan ist seit vielen Jahren ein stabilisierender Faktor in Zentralasien. Das politische und wirtschaftliche Umfeld hängt von einer soliden und effektiven Nachfolgeplanung für den politischen Führer des Landes ab. Erste wichtige Schritte wurden ergriffen, um Parlament und Regierung zu stärken und einen positiven Übergang in 2020 und Folgejahre zu erleichtern. Darüber hinaus sollte die *Belt & Road Initiative,* allgemein bekannt als *Seidenstraße-Initiative,* riesige Infrastrukturinvestitionen mit sich bringen. Das AIFC ist eine Säule für ihre Finanzierung. Mit konstant hohen Auslandsinvestitionen in Höhe von USD 27 Mrd. p. a., bei kontinuierlicher internationaler Zusammenarbeit, fortdauerndem Investment in das Humankapital, Ausbau des AIFC, und auch unter Berücksichtigung der *Belt & Road Initiative* ist Kasachstans Zukunft sehr viel versprechend.

(Übersetzung aus dem Englischen: S. Mueller)

Peter Tils
peter-a.tils@db.com

Teil 2

Modernes Kasachstan
– attraktives Investmentziel

EAWU und Neue Seidenstraße bieten langfristige, hervorragende Marktchancen und machen Kasachstan zu einem idealen Standort für deutsche Unternehmen

Interview mit Herrn Dr. Robert Breitner, Delegierter der Deutschen Wirtschaft für Zentralasien mit Sitz in Almaty

CCP: *Unser Thema ist das moderne Kasachstan. Sie, Herr Dr. Breitner, leben vor Ort und sehen die Entwicklung. Nennen Sie doch bitte die Ihrer Meinung nach charakteristischen Merkmale des modernen, heutigen Kasachstan.*

RB: 1. Ambitioniert: 2013 verkündete Präsident Nasarbajew die *Strategie Kasachstan 2050*. Diese benennt die langfristigen Vorgaben für die Entwicklung von Kasachstan. Das Ziel der Strategie ist der Aufstieg des Landes in die Gruppe der 30 am meisten entwickelten Staaten. Die Eckpfeiler der kasachischen Wirtschafts- und Finanzpolitik sollen eine geringe Verschuldung und eine Neuausrichtung der Energieversorgung, eine verstärkte Modernisierung und Diversifizierung der kasachischen Wirtschaft sei. Damit soll der Abbau und Weiterverarbeitung von Rohstoffen erweitert und die Abhängigkeit von Rohöl verringert werden. Besondere Schwerpunkte sind der Ausbau der verarbeitenden Industrie, der Landwirtschaft und des Transportwesens, der Umstrukturierung des Energiesektors und die Förderung von mittelständischen Unternehmen.

Das starke Engagement von Kasachstan um gute wirtschaftspolitische Rahmenbedingungen wird im *Doing Business Ranking der Weltbank* gewürdigt, bei dem Kasachstan Platz 35 einnahm und damit zur Spitzengruppe der GUS-Länder gehört.

2. Internationale Ausrichtung: Die wichtigsten direkten Handelspartner von Kasachstan sind China und Russland. Kasachstan ist das Gründungsmitglied der *Eurasischen Wirtschaftsunion (EAWU)*, ist Mitglied der *Shanghai Organisation für Zusammenarbeit* und beteiligt sich

aktiv an der chinesischen Initiative *One Belt, One Road*, der Neuen Seidenstraße.

CCP: *Kasachstan ist durch seine Lage in Zentralasien, zwischen China und Russland, ein sehr interessanter Standort für ausländische Investoren. Welchen Platz nimmt Deutschland insgesamt zurzeit als Investor in Kasachstan ein, im Verhältnis zur Gesamtheit von Investoren anderer Länder?*

RB: Fast die Hälfte aller bisher getätigten ausländischen Direktinvestitionen stammte Ende 2017 aus den Niederlanden. Ein Grund hierfür ist, dass viele ausländische Unternehmen ihre Investitionen in Kasachstan über niederländische Holdings abwickeln. Deutschland lag mit Direktinvestitionen in Höhe von 558 Millionen US-Dollar auf Platz 17. Laut Angaben der Bundesbank lagen die von 40 Unternehmen getragenen deutschen Direktinvestitionen in Kasachstan Ende 2016 bei 225 Millionen Euro.

CCP: *Welche deutschen Firmen sind schon am längsten in Kasachstan mit Produktionsanlagen, und gewiss aus gutem Grund.*

RB: Zu den am längsten bereits produzierenden deutschen Unternehmen gehören folgende Mitgliedsunternehmen des Verbandes der deutschen Wirtschaft in Kasachstan: KNAUF, Henkel, BASF, Böhmer Armaturen, Isoplus, ODDESSE (OZA) und zeitnah WILO.

CCP: *Die großen deutschen Namen sind überall in der Welt die ersten deutschen Investoren, jedoch der deutsche Mittelstand ist das Rückgrat der deutschen Wirtschaft und ebenfalls weltweit geschätzt. In welchem Maße ist er zurzeit in Kasachstan präsent?*

RB: Fünf der sieben gerade genannten produzierenden Unternehmen sind mittelständische, die in Kasachstan für Zentralasien, die Mongolei und teilweise auch den Südkaukasus produzieren und dafür Kasachstan als Standort ausgewählt haben. Darüber hinaus findet man unter den circa 100 Mitgliedsunternehmen des Verbandes der deutschen Wirtschaft in Kasachstan weitere circa 70 Prozent mittelständische deutsche Unternehmen, die vor allem mit Repräsentanzen in Kasachstan vertreten sind.

CCP: *Was macht Kasachstan heute als Investitionsziel und Standort für deutsche mittelständische Firmen interessant?*

RB: Kasachstan besitzt die leistungsfähigste Volkswirtschaft in Zentralasien, günstige Personalkosten und hat selbst einen hohen Modernisierungsbedarf. Darüber hinaus liegt das Land zwischen China und

Russland an der *Neuen Seidenstraße* und ist Mitglied der EAWU, was auch mittelständischen Unternehmen neue und bislang vollkommen unerschlossene Marktchancen bietet.

CCP: *Was schätzt man in Kasachstan an deutschen mittelständischen Unternehmen?*

RB: Vor allem deren hochspezialisierten Produkte und Dienstleistungen. Außerdem schätzt man deren langfristig angelegtes wirtschaftliches, aber auch soziales Engagement für deren Mitarbeiter und die Regionen, in denen sie tätig sind.

CCP: *Nennen Sie doch bitte einige Projekte, die in den letzten 3-5 Jahren von deutschen mittelständischen Firmen realisiert wurden und wesentlich zum Image des Landes als modern beigetragen haben.*

RB: Der Autobahnbau in Kasachstan von Astana nach Borovoe durch die GP Papenburg Baugesellschaft mbH oder ein 4 km langer unterirdische Schacht von insgesamt 12 km für den Chromerzabbau im Nordwesten des Landes durch die TOO SCHACHTBAU Kasachstan.

CCP: *In welchen Sektoren der Wirtschaft Kasachstans ist der innovative deutsche Mittelstand zurzeit in Kasachstan sehr gefragt?*

RB: Aufgrund der großen geographischen Ausdehnung Kasachstans und des Modernisierungsbedarfs, ist das Land vor allem interessant für Spezialanbieter von Bahn-, Hafen-, Flug- und Straßenbautechnik, jedoch auch für Anbieter zur Erschließung und Erweiterung von Erdöl und Erdgas, Pipeline- und Kraftwerkstechnik sowie für Logistikunternehmen. Außerdem möchte sich Kasachstan schrittweise unabhängiger von Agrar- und Nahrungsmittelimporten machen und setzt hier auf mehr lokal produzierte Nahrungsmittel. Daher ist Kasachstan auch interessant für die Produzenten von Nahrungsmitteln und Maschinen dafür. Für diesen Sektor spricht auch die regionale Nähe zu China als möglichen weiteren Exportmarkt.

CCP: *Was sollten deutsche Führungskräfte, die in nächster Zukunft nach Kasachstan delegiert werden, wissen resp. können und tun oder nicht tun, um von Anfang an Erfolg zu haben in diesem kulturell so andersartigen Land, im Vergleich zu Deutschland?*

RB: Um möglichst selbstständig in Kasachstan und Zentralasien arbeiten zu können, sollte man Geduld haben, zuhören können und mit Mitarbeitern und Partnern soziale Kontakte pflegen. Jedes Geschäft in

Kasachstan, wie auch überall in der Welt, beginnt mit guten persönlichen Beziehungen und die Kenntnis der Sprache von Partnern und Mitarbeitern ist ein großer Vorteil dabei.

CCP: *Alle Geschäftsleute haben auch ein persönliches Leben und Interesse. Daher sind auch Ihre persönlichen Erfahrungen interessant. Also, was gefällt Ihnen persönlich an Ihrem Leben in Almaty und in Kasachstan?*

RB: Ich bin erst sehr kurze Zeit in Kasachstan und lebe in Almaty. Dort schätze ich sehr die Berge, die zu jeder Jahreszeit Möglichkeiten für die Freizeit bieten, besonders zum Wandern und Ski fahren.

CCP: *Vielen Dank, Herr Dr. Breitner, für dieses Gespräch. Sicherlich gibt es künftigen deutschen Investoren interessante Einblicke und motivierende Impulse für das moderne Kasachstan als Investitionsziel.*

Delegation der Deutschen Wirtschaft für Zentralasien
Businesszentrum «Koktem Square»
Bostandykski rayon
Mkr. Koktem 1, dom 15 a
050040 Almaty, Kasachstan
✆ +7 727 35610 - 61, 62, 63, 64, 65
✉ info@ahk-za.com

Delegation der Deutschen
Wirtschaft für Zentralasien
Представительство Германской
экономики в Центральной Азии

Hervorragende Chancen für Investoren in Kasachstan

Von Hans-Joachim Bischoff,
INVEST KAZAKH Representative
Germany

Kasachstan, das neuntgrößte Land der Erde, hat eine zentrale Lage an der historischen Seidenstraße inne. Das Interesse an den wirtschaftlichen Beziehungen mit Kasachstan wächst stetig, da der Standort vorteilhafte Bedingungen für Investoren und günstige Handelsrouten bietet. Ein Investor kann beispielsweise eine staatliche Investitionsförderung von bis zu 30 Prozent erhalten, und auch die im Programm des Präsidenten beschriebenen Schritte zur Diversifizierung der Wirtschaft stellen eine langfristige und zuverlässige Strategie dar.
Noch im Jahr 2016 stand Kasachstan vor Herausforderungen im Zusammenhang mit niedrigen Rohstoffpreisen. Durch die von der kasachischen Regierung durchgeführten fiskalpolitischen Unterstützungsmaßnahmen und Strukturreformen ist es gelungen, die Wirtschaftslage zu verbessern. Der Regenerationsprozess für die kasachische Wirtschaft wurde aktiviert. Als Folge hat das BIP-Wachstum im Jahr 2017 vier Prozent erreicht.

Geschäftsklima deutlich verbessert

2017 hatte sich der Handel zwischen Deutschland und der Region spürbar intensiviert: Das bilaterale Handelsvolumen mit Kasachstan kletterte um 23 Prozent auf rund fünf Milliarden Euro. Kasachstan ist für die deutschen Unternehmen der wichtigste Wirtschaftspartner in der Region Zentralasien. Trotz seines Rohstoffreichtums verfolgt das Land eine klare Modernisierungsstrategie. Bei der technischen und innovativen Erneuerung werden vor allem deutsche Unternehmen als Wunschpartner gesehen.
Seit 2017 ist in Kasachstan das Staatsunternehmen KAZAKH INVEST für Maßnahmen der staatlichen Unterstützung für industrielle und innovative Prozesse sowie zur Investorenanwerbung und Standortmarketing zuständig.

Über Kasachstan

Name:	Republik Kasachstan
Gründungsjahr:	1991, 16. Dezember
Regierungssystem:	Einheitlicher Staat mit Präsidialsystem
Präsident:	Nursultan Nazarbajev
Amtssprachen:	Kasachisch (Staatssprache) und Russisch
Hauptstadt:	Astana
Landfläche:	2 717 300 km² (9.-größtes Land der Erde)
Verwaltungseinheiten:	14 Regionen 3 Städte nationaler Bedeutung: Astana (ca. 1 Mio. Einwohner) Almaty (ca. 1,7 Mio. Einwohner) Schymkent (ca. 1 Mio. Einwohner)
Bevölkerung:	ca. 18 Mio.
Bevölkerungsdichte:	ca. 7 Einwohner/km²
Währung:	Tenge (KZT) 1 KZT – 0,00245336EUR; 1 EUR – 407,604 KZT
Zeitzone:	GMT West/East + 5/+6
Internationale Telefonvorwahl:	+7
Internet Code:	.kz
Internationaler Landescode:	KZ
Nationalfeiertag:	16. Dezember

Mit einem neuen Strategiepaket strebt Kasachstan nach der Steigerung der Industrieexporte. Darüber hinaus treibt das Land die Digitalisierung der Wirtschaft auf Basis des Programms *Digitalisierung Kasachstans* voran. Trotz der starken Abhängigkeit von Rohstoffpreisen wird ein Wirtschaftswachstum gemäß der soziowirtschaftlichen Prognose 2018-2022 von 3,1 bis 4,2 Prozent erwartet.
Es wird sich auf Basis der gemäßigten Wachstumsraten der Weltwirtschaft, des Wiederanstiegs der Nachfrage sowie der Aufrechterhaltung niedriger Rohstoffpreise entwickeln. Kasachstan bleibt zudem weiterhin der mit Abstand größte Wirtschaftspartner Deutschlands in Zentralasien.
Die Aufrechterhaltung eines günstigen Investitionsklimas und die Förderung der ausländischen Direktinvestitionen in die Wirtschaft sind zwei der wichtigsten Aufgaben. Ziel des Staatsprogramms für industrielle und innovative Entwicklung der Republik Kasachstan im Zeitraum von 2015 bis 2019 ist es, eine auf Arbeitsproduktivität und Aufstieg der Exportvolumen der verarbeiteten Erzeugnisse orientierte Wettbewerbsfähigkeit der Verarbeitungsindustrie zu fördern.
Eine bedeutende Rolle spielt die Heranziehung von Investitionen – einschließlich ausländischer.
Ausländische Direktinvestitionen sind hauptsächlich auf die Bereiche Chemie- und Pharmazieindustrie, Maschinenbau, Bauwesen, Transportwesen und Bergbau von Metallerzen gerichtet.
Lohnend ist nach wie vor die Förderung und Verarbeitung der Bodenschätze des Landes, vor allem von Erdöl und Gas, jedoch auch von Uran, Kupfer, Zink, Eisenerz und anderen. Laut der Einschätzungen von *Trading Economics* werden Investitionen in Höhe von 5,5 Mrd. USD im 2. Quartal 2018 erwartet. Schon im 1. Quartal 2018 sind 5,16 Mrd. USD investiert worden.
Auch die Landwirtschaft und die Nahrungsmittelindustrie sind gefragt. Zudem bergen auch die Energiewirtschaft und der Handel Potenzial für deutsche Investoren.

Digitalisierung
als Triebkraft der deutsch-kasachischen Beziehungen

Kasachstan möchte bis 2050 zu den 30 wirtschaftsstärksten Ländern der Welt gehören. Dafür wäre ein jährliches Wachstum von rund fünf Prozent notwendig. Allein mit dem Rohstoffreichtum, mit dem das größte

Anhaltend hohes Wachstum

Der Internationale Währungsfonds (IWF) gab eine optimistische Prognose für das BIP-Wachstum in Kasachstan.

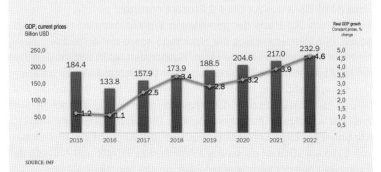

SOURCE: IMF

Warum In Kasachstan investieren?

GESCHÄFTS-FREUNDLICHE UMGEBUNG

SOZIALE / WIRTSCHAFTLICHE STABILITÄT

ATTRAKTIVITÄT FÜR INVESTITIONEN

NACHHALTIG HOHES WACHSTUM

EINKOMMENS GLEICHHEIT

GÜNSTIGE STEUERREGELUNG

ZUGANG ZU DEN WICHTIGSTEN REGIONALMÄRKTEN

ERFAHRENE UND AUSGEBILDETE ARBEITSKRÄFTE

STAATLICHE UNTERSTÜTZUNG

zentralasiatische Land gesegnet ist, wäre dieses Ziel nicht zu erreichen. Daher setzt die kasachische Regierung auf weitere Wachstumstreiber, darunter – dem Zeitgeist entsprechend – auch auf Digitalisierung.

Die Industriebranchen, allen voran der Bergbau und die Schwerindustrie, sollen durch die Industrie 4.0 wettbewerbsstärker und profitabler gemacht werden.

Folgendes ist bei Investitionen in Kasachstan zu beachten:

1. Information

Zunächst empfiehlt sich ein Gespräch mit KAZAKH INVEST. Als Ansprechpartner in Deutschland steht *Hans-Joachim Bischoff* zur Verfügung.

2. Zahlungsprozesse mit kasachischen Banken

Augenmerk sollten deutsche Unternehmen auf die Abwicklung von Zahlungen legen. Allein die Prozedur der Eröffnung eines Bankkontos kann mehrere Wochen in Anspruch nehmen und einen erheblichen Aufwand für die notarielle Beglaubigung von Unterschriftskarten, Übersendung der elektronischen Signaturvorrichtungen etc. beanspruchen.

Kasachische Banken fordern aus Gründen der Devisenregulierung oft Kopien von Verträgen oder Rechnungen an, um die Zahlung auszuführen. Deshalb muss stets berücksichtigt werden, dass eine Zahlung nicht von heute auf morgen abgewickelt werden kann, besonders dann, wenn Mitarbeiter aus dem Kontrollbereich die Zahlung als Zweiunterschriftsberechtigte freigeben müssen. Wegen des Zeitunterschiedes von vier bis fünf Stunden müssen solche Zahlungsvorgänge geplant und eng mit dem Tochterunternehmen abgestimmt werden.

3. Zollgesetzbuch der Eurasischen Wirtschaftsunion
(EAWU-ZGB)

Am 1. Januar 2018 ist das neue Zollgesetzbuch der *Eurasischen Wirtschaftsunion* (kurz EAWU-ZGB) in Kraft getreten.

Grundlage sind fortschrittliche Praktiken des Zollwesens, einschließlich der Vorschriften des *Übereinkommens von Kyoto* über die Vereinfachung der Harmonisierung der Zollverfahren und der *Bali-Vereinbarung der Welthandelsorganisation* über die Vereinfachung der Handelsverfahren.

Modern Kazakhstan

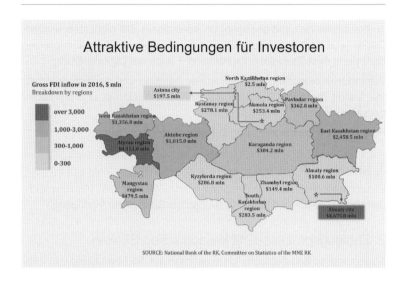

Ein wichtiger Vorteil besteht darin, dass klare und deutliche Rechtsverhältnisse festgelegt wurden. Auf diese Weise kennt jeder Wirtschaftsteilnehmer seine Rechte und Pflichten. Subjektivität wurde bei der Entscheidungsfindung der Zollbehörden ausgeschlossen, unter anderem durch den Einsatz von Informationssystemen und -technologien. Auch Kollisionen in den Rechtsvorschriften, sowohl direkt im Zollbereich wie auch in anderen Bereichen der Gesetzgebung wurden ausgeschlossen, da jede Unklarheit für Investoren zu finanziellen Verlusten führen kann, die auf das Ergebnis eines Projekts starke Auswirkungen haben können. Das EAWU-ZGB hat finanzielle Risiken in Bezug auf Steuern und Strafen minimiert.

Es wird erwartet, dass der innovative Charakter des EAWU-ZGB zu einem Handelsvolumenanstieg führt und die Entwicklung der Unionswirtschaft fördert.

4. Verbesserungen der Investitionsbedingungen

Viele internationale Unternehmen kommen gerade jetzt nach Kasachstan. Aufgrund von drastisch gefallenen Strukturkosten und relativ leichten rechtlichen Rahmenbedingungen zieht das Land die Aufmerksamkeit ausländischer Firmen auf sich.

Heutzutage richtet sich die kasachische Regierung nach Programmen

wie zum Beispiel *Nurly Zhol* und *Digitalisierung Kasachstans*, die die Wirtschaftsentwicklung forcieren sollten.
Außerdem werden Verbesserungen des Investitionsklimas, des Konkurrenzumfeldes und der Förderung der Innovationsaktivität im Rahmen der Umsetzung des *Nationsplans 100 konkrete Schritte* erwartet.
Der Privatsektor muss einer der Hauptquellen des Wirtschaftswachstums sein. Dazu werden Maßnahmen zur Senkung aller Kostenarten für eine Geschäftsführung getroffen. Erbringungsverfahren der Staatsdienstleistungen werden möglichst optimiert und digitalisiert.
Um das Geschäftsumfeld zu verbessern, sind Reformen von Steuer- und Zollgesetzten eingeplant. Darüber hinaus werden Verfahren der Geschäftseröffnung und Eigentumsregistrierung vereinfacht sowie die Minderheitsinvestorenrechte verstärkt.
Fazit: Bei großer Abhängigkeit von Rohstoffexporten ist Kasachstan generell auf einem sehr guten Weg einer positiven Wirtschafts- und politischen Entwicklung.

5. Eröffnung des Astana International Financial Centre (AIFC)

Mit Jahresbeginn startete das *Astana International Financial Centre* (AIFC) seinen Betrieb. Der unter Schirmherrschaft von Präsident Nursultan Nasarbajew agierende Finanzhub ist Teil der Strategie Kasachstans, einen Platz unter den dreißig größten Wirtschaftsnationen der Welt zu bekommen. Das neue Finanzzentrum hat seinen Sitz auf dem modernen Gelände der Weltausstellung Expo 2017 in der Hauptstadt Astana.
Von Interessenvertretungen der deutschen Wirtschaft wurde die Gründung des Finanzzentrums begrüßt. Michael Harms, Geschäftsführer des Ost-Ausschusses der Deutschen Wirtschaft, sagte in einem Interview: „Deutsche Unternehmen könnten viel mehr in Kasachstan investieren. Wir müssen noch härter daran arbeiten, gemeinsame Projekte zu erschaffen." Für die deutsche Wirtschaft sei es wichtig, Investoren zu unterstützen und für stabile Geschäftsbedingungen zu sorgen. Dem Finanzzentrum komme dabei eine Schlüsselrolle für künftige ausländische Investitionen zu.
Die ausländischen Direktinvestitionen in Kasachstan – sie betrugen im Jahr 2017 bereits 5 381 Milliarden US-Dollar – ließen die postsowjetische Republik nach dem *Doing-Business-Index* bereits auf Platz 36 von 190 erscheinen.

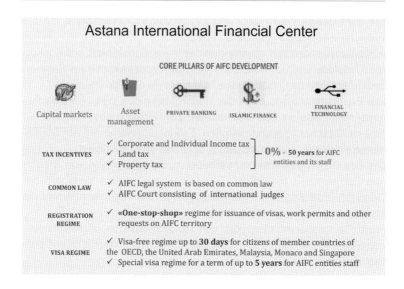

Ziel des *Internationalen Finanzzentrums* ist es, als eine den internationalen Standards entsprechende Institution die Beziehungen zwischen angesiedelten Unternehmen nach den Prinzipien des Common Law zu regeln. Dafür soll zudem ein Finanzgericht geschaffen werden, das auch für Streitigkeiten und bei Fragen zum Thema Investitionen zuständig ist.

Geplante Vergünstigungen für ausländische Unternehmen bei Ansiedlung in Kasachstan:

- Befreiung von der Körperschaftsteuer,
- Befreiung von der Einkommensteuer für dort ansässige Arbeitnehmer,
- Erstattung der Umsatzsteuer für ausländische Mitarbeiter und
- Abschaffung der Arbeitsgenehmigungspflicht für ausländische Mitarbeiter.

Für 2018 sind weitreichende Privatisierungsvorhaben angelaufen.

Das AIFC soll ab sofort das Zentrum für Anziehung von Investitionen sein und einen respektablen Platz im internationalen Finanzsystem einnehmen.

Hans-Joachim Bischoff ist seit 01.01.2018 Repräsentant von KAZAKH INVEST in Deutschland. KAZAKH INVEST bietet Dienstleistungen zur Unterstützung von Investitionsprojekten in Kasachstan, von der Idee bis zur Umsetzung nach dem Prinzip „One-Stop-Shop" und ist für Investoren kostenfrei.

Hans-Joachim Bischoff bekleidete in seiner bisherigen Karriere verschiedene Vorstandspositionen und ist Geschäftsführer der NEXT STEP Personal in Hannover.

Seine Karriere begann mit Management Positionen bei Finanzmarkt- und Online- Kommunikationsunternehmen mit nationaler und internationaler Ausrichtung. Dabei unterstützte der Kommunikationsexperte durch seine profunden Kenntnisse auf den Gebieten der Finanz-Kommunikation und Investor Relations.

Besonders erfolgreich gestalteten sich diverse Investitionen und internationale Investitionsprojekte in Deutschland und Südafrika.

Er verantwortete erfolgreich mehrere Börsengänge und Kapitalerhöhungen von börsennotierten Unternehmen als *Head of Investor Relations*.

Hans-Joachim Bischoff
INVEST KAZAKH Representative Germany
KAZAKH INVEST National Company JSC

Germany Office:

Krackeweg 6, 30559 Hannover, Germany

Kazakhstan Office:

2 Kunayev st., 7th floor,
Astana, Kazakhstan 010000
- ✆ + 49 511 300 89 90
- 🔊 + 49 178 72 58 68 0
- ✉ bischoff@invest.gov.kz
- 🌐 www.invest.gov.kz

Rechtliche Grundlagen für Geschäfte mit kasachischen Partnern

Von Prof. Dr. Hans-Joachim Schramm und Dimitri Olejnik, Ostinstitut Wismar

1. Die kasachische Rechtsordnung

Die kasachische Rechtsordnung beruht auf der Verfassung vom 30. August 1995, die im Wege eines Referendums angenommen wurde. Sie enthält alle diejenigen Institutionen und Konzepte, die man auch in den entsprechenden Dokumenten westlicher Staaten findet:
- Grundrechte,
- Gewaltenteilung,
- Rechtsstaatlichkeit,
- Demokratie,
- unabhängige Justiz und
- Sozialstaatlichkeit.

Immerhin nimmt Kasachstan im *World Justice Report 2017-2018* unter allen Nachfolgestaaten der Sowjetunion nach Georgien in puncto Rechtsstaatlichkeit den zweitbesten Platz ein. In wirtschaftlicher Hinsicht betont die Verfassung einerseits das Recht auf freie unternehmerische Betätigung, andererseits das fortbestehende Staatseigentum an Boden und Bodenschätzen. Diesen Regelungen entspricht der von Autoren der Weltbank bestätigte Befund, dass sich in Kasachstan weiterhin ein großer Teil der Unternehmen, insbesondere in den zentralen Sektoren Bodenschätze, Energie, Transport, Wasser und Kommunikation, in staatlicher Hand befindet.

2. Das kasachische Wirtschaftsrecht

Im Wirtschaftsrecht lässt sich eine starke *Orientierung am russischen Recht* ausmachen, die in jüngerer Zeit etwas durch angelsächsische Einflüsse überlagert wird. Die Orientierung am russischen Recht hat ihre Grundlagen in den engen Bindungen beider Länder, sowohl in kultureller als auch in wirtschaftlicher Hinsicht. Mittelbar führt das dazu,

dass viele Institute des kasachischen Rechts einem deutschen Juristen durchaus vertraut sind, weil die Schöpfer des russischen Zivilrechts ihrerseits starke Anleihen am deutschen Recht genommen haben.
Herausragendes Symbol dieser engen Verbindung mit dem russischen Recht ist *das kasachische Zivilgesetzbuch vom 27.12.1994* (Teil 1) und vom 1.7.1999 (Teil 2), das dem russischen Zivilgesetzbuch anverwandt ist. Darin findet sich auch ein deutscher Jurist trotz Unterschieden im Detail zurecht. Hier sind die grundlegenden Vertrags- und sachrechtlichen Normen niedergelegt und darüber hinaus, insoweit abweichend vom deutschen BGB, auch die *Bestimmungen zum intellektuellen Eigentum* und zum *Kollisionsrecht* (internationales Privatrecht). Festzustellen ist jedoch ein zunehmendes Ausweichen auf Spezialgesetze, etwa im Bereich des *Verbraucherschutzes,* der *Bankverträge* oder der *Kreditsicherheiten.* Letztere gibt es in Kasachstan vor allem in Form des *Pfandrechts* und der *Hypothek.*
Rechte an Grund und Boden sind im *Bodengesetzbuch* niedergelegt. Bemerkenswert ist in dieser Hinsicht, dass Kasachstan im *Doing Business Report 2018 (DBR 2018)* der Weltbank im Hinblick auf die Durchsetzung von Verträgen und Registrierung von Eigentum überdurchschnittlich gut abschneidet.

3. Gesellschafts- und Kapitalmarkrecht unter US-amerikanischem Einfluss

Der *starke US-amerikanische Einfluss* kommt vorrangig im *Gesellschafts-* und *Kapitalmarktrecht* zum Ausdruck. Zentrale gesellschaftsrechtliche Regelung ist das *Gesetz über Aktiengesellschaften* vom 13.05.2003, das stark an das Vorbild einer US-amerikanischen Corporation angelehnt ist. Allerdings ist das Mindestkapital einer kasachischen Aktiengesellschaft im internationalen Vergleich mit über 340 000 USD hoch angesetzt. Immerhin hat dieses Gesetz Kasachstan die beste Bewertung weltweit im DBR2018 in der Kategorie *Schutz von Minderheitsgesellschaftern* eingebracht.
Für mittelständische Investoren kommt allerdings eher das Pendant zur GmbH in Betracht, das in Kasachstan unter der Bezeichnung *Genossenschaft (tovarishtshestvo) mit beschränkter Haftung* firmiert und im Gesetz vom 22.04.1998 geregelt ist (Gesetz TOO). Wie die abweichende Bezeichnung bereits andeutet, ist diese Rechtsform nur bedingt mit einer GmbH in Deutschland gleichzusetzen, da die Gesellschafter bei einer Unterbilanz von den Gläubigern in Anspruch genommen werden

können (Art. 25 Abs.3 Gesetz TOO). Ein Registerwesen gibt es, doch ist dessen Funktion nicht mit der eines Handelsregisters gleichzusetzen. Offenkundigstes Zeichen der Anlehnung an angelsächsische Vorbilder ist die Schaffung des *Astana Internationalen Finanzzentrums* durch das gleichlautende Gesetz vom 7.12.2015. Hier wird der Versuch unternommen, die Hauptstadt Astana zu einem regionalen Finanzzentrum auszubauen, insbesondere dadurch, dass eine *Sonderwirtschaftszone in der Hauptstadt Astana* eingerichtet wurde, die man der Jurisdiktion der kasachischen Justiz entzogen hat. Stattdessen gilt in dieser Enklave das Recht von England und Wales und die Rechtsprechung ist englischen Richtern übertragen. Ob dies ein Schritt in die richtige Richtung war, wird sich erst noch erweisen müssen.

4. Das kasachische Unternehmensgesetzbuch

Die wesentlichen *Bestimmungen zum Wirtschaftsverwaltungsrecht* sind im *Unternehmensgesetzbuch* vom 29.10.2015 niedergelegt, das unter anderem allgemeine Bestimmungen zum Regulierungs-, Wettbewerbs-, Kartell- und Subventionsrecht enthält. Das allgemeine Gewerberecht war bereits ein Jahr zuvor in Gestalt des *Gesetzes über Genehmigungen und Anzeigen* am 16.05.2014 grundlegend reformiert worden. Allerdings lässt sich dem DBR2018 fortbestehender Reformbedarf entnehmen, denn im Hinblick auf das Verfahren zur Gründung von Unternehmen und dem Erwerb einer Baugenehmigung erzielt Kasachstan lediglich eine Bewertung im Mittelfeld. Erwähnung verdient zudem das *Gesetz über Bodenschätze und Nutzung von Bodenschätzen* vom 24.6.2010, das am 11.7.2017 grundlegend überarbeitet wurde. In diesem Gesetz finden sich die einschlägigen Regelungen im Hinblick auf die Exploration und Ausbeutung von Rohstoffen, die in dem Land in großem Maße vorhanden sind. Die *Währungsgesetzgebung* wie auch das *Aufenthaltsrecht für ausländische Investoren* sind liberal.

5. Die Qualität der Gerichte

Die *Qualität der Gerichte* gehört weiterhin zu den „Baustellen" der Reform, trotz beachtlicher Fortschritte. Auf der anderen Seite genießt die *Reform der Justiz* mit dem Ziel der Stärkung der Unabhängigkeit der Richter und der *Einführung von Verwaltungsgerichten* hohe Priorität. In diesem Zusammenhang steht weiter, dass die Bezahlung der

Richter in letzter Zeit spürbar erhöht wurde. So verdient ein Richter der Eingangsinstanz ca. 500 USD im Monat, was den Richterberuf vergleichsweise attraktiv macht. Anders als in vielen Ländern gibt es in Kasachstan kein Verfassungsgericht, sondern einen *Verfassungsrat*, der aber gleichwohl Gesetze im Wege der konkreten Normenkontrolle für verfassungswidrig erklären kann.

Ausländischen Investoren bleibt demgegenüber die Möglichkeit des Ausweichens auf *Schiedsgerichte*. Die einschlägigen Normen finden sich im *Gesetz über die Schiedsgerichtsbarkeit* vom 8.4.2016. Eine Vollstreckung von Schiedssprüchen in Kasachstan ist möglich, da dort seit 1996 *die New Yorker Konvention über die Anerkennung und Vollstreckung internationaler Schiedssprüche* gilt.

6. Außenwirtschaft: Mitgliedschaft in der WTO und der EAWU

In außenwirtschaftlicher Hinsicht ist bedeutsam, dass Kasachstan am 30.11.2015 in die WTO aufgenommen wurde, gleichzeitig aber Mitglied der von Russland dominierten *Eurasischen Wirtschaftsunion* (EAWU) ist, die zum 1.1.2015 ins Leben gerufen wurde. Zu letzterer gehören neben Russland und Kasachstan noch Armenien, Weißrussland und Kirgisistan. Zentraler Regelungsgehalt der *Eurasischen Wirtschaftsunion* ist die Schaffung einer Zollunion, vergleichbar mit der EWG in ihrer frühen Phase. Strukturell ist die *Eurasische Union* jedoch nur eingeschränkt mit der *Europäischen Union* vergleichbar. Das UN-Kaufrecht hat Kasachstan noch nicht als für sich verbindlich akzeptiert. Ist die Geltung bei internationalen Kaufverträgen erwünscht, so sollte dies ausdrücklich vereinbart werden.

7. Programm der 100 konkreten Schritte und Strategie bis 2025

Im Bereich der Korruptionsbekämpfung macht Kasachstan ebenfalls Fortschritte, auch wenn die Bemühungen weiter fortgesetzt werden müssen. Im Ranking von *Transparency International* sind die Ergebnisse des Jahres 2017 die besten bisher erzielten. Positiv zu vermerken sind vor allem die Verabschiedung neuer Anti-Korruptionsgesetze, die Schaffung öffentlicher Kontrollmechanismen und Verbesserungen im Bereich des Vergaberechts.

Vor diesem Hintergrund sind die jüngsten Reformprogramme zu sehen. So wurde im Mai 2015 das von der Regierung erarbeitete *Programm der 100 konkreten Schritte* verabschiedet. Jüngste Maßnahme ist der

Ukaz vom 15.2.2018, mit dem die *Entwicklungsstrategie bis 2025* bestätigt wurde. Neu hinzugekommen ist hier der Schwerpunkt *Digitalisierung* während die *führende Rolle des staatlichen Sektors bei der Umsetzung der Reformen* bestätigt wurde.

Prof. Dr. Hans-Joachim Schramm
joachim.schramm@ostinstitut.de

Teil 3

Deutsche Firmen formen das moderne Kasachstan mit

Modernes Kasachstan

BASF in Zentralasien

Schlüsselindustrien
Landwirtschaft
Bauwesen
Automotive Industrie
Öl & Gas
Bergbau

Schlüsselzahlen
~ 120 Mitarbeiter
2 Produktionsanlagen
für Bauchemikalien
in Almaty und Astana

BASF Central Asia LLP

Der BASF Zentralasien LLP Hauptsitz befindet sich in Almaty und bildet ein regionales Zentrum für die Märkte von Kasachstan, Kirgisistan, Tadschikistan, Turkmenistan und Usbekistan. Das Unternehmen arbeitet aktiv in Zentralasien und feierte im Jahre 2017 sein 25-jähriges Jubiläum in Kasachstan und Usbekistan. In den vergangenen Jahren erwarb BASF in Zentralasien den Ruf eines starken Partners und eines zuverlässigen Herstellers von qualitativ hochwertigen Materialien und Lösungen.

Über BASF

BASF produziert Chemie für eine nachhaltige Zukunft. Wir verbinden wirtschaftlichen Erfolg mit Umweltschutz und sozialer Verantwortung. Die mehr als 115 000 Mitarbeiter in der BASF-Gruppe arbeiten für einen Beitrag zum Erfolg unserer Kunden in nahezu allen Branchen und in fast jedem Land der Welt. Unser Portfolio gliedert sich in fünf Segmente: Chemikalien, Performance Produkte, funktionale Materialien & Lösungen, Lösungen für die Landwirtschaft und Öl & Gas. In 2017 generierte BASF einen Umsatz von € 64,5 Milliarden. BASF Aktien werden an den Börsen in Frankfurt (BAS), London (BFA) und Zürich (BAS) gehandelt. Weitere Informationen unter www.basf.com.

(Aus dem Englischen übersetzt von S. Mueller)

BASF Central Asia LLP
050016, Rayimbek ave., 211A
Almaty, Kazakhstan

Kontakt:

Rashid Kabykayev
Manager corporate communications and government relations
LLP BASF Central Asia,
3A, Charles De Gaulle,
010000 Astana, Kazakhstan

📞 +7 7172 27 04 40-110,
📶 +7 701 029 67 38,
✉ rashid.kabykayev@basf.com

BASF: Kundennähe und Entwicklung lokaler Talente

Interview mit Frau Saule Baitzhaunova, Managing Director, BASF Central Asia LLP

CCP: *BASF-Zentralasien unterhält Niederlassungen und Produktionsstätten in verschiedenen Ländern und Orten in Zentralasien. Das bedeutet, innerhalb Ihres Unternehmens haben Sie es mit verschiedenen asiatischen Kulturen zu tun; die Management-Herausforderung scheint ziemlich bedeutend. Welche Führungsgrundsätze praktizieren Sie an Ihrem BASF-Standort in Kasachstan, die gleichen wie in der deutschen Zentrale oder die üblichen in Kasachstan und andere in den anderen zentralasiatischen Ländern?*

SB: Die kulturelle Vielfalt in unserer Region empfinde ich nicht als Herausforderung. Im Gegenteil, das ist eine einzigartige Gelegenheit, unsere Führungskompetenzen zu beweisen, durch Kontaktaufnahme und Arbeit mit Menschen aus verschiedenen Kulturen und Regionen. Natürlich sind wir den allgemeinen BASF Führungsprinzipien verpflichtet, jedoch wir respektieren auch die kulturellen und lokalen Besonderheiten eines aufstrebenden Marktes.

CCP: *Wie sieht Ihr Führungsteam in Kasachstan aus: Ist es ein lokales Management-Team oder ein internationales Team mit deutscher Beteiligung?*

SB: Unser Unternehmen versteht die kulturellen Besonderheiten unserer Region, und die Bedeutung von Nähe und lokaler Entwicklung; das heißt, BASF setzt auf die Entwicklung lokaler Mitarbeiter und Talente. Unser Management-Team besteht aus kasachischen, usbekischen, turkmenischen und ukrainischen Kollegen.

CCP: *Wenn die Mitglieder des Management-Teams verschiedene kulturelle Backgrounds haben, existieren da nicht verschiedene Erwartungen an den Führungsstil und die Problemlösung in dem Werk in Kasachstan?*

SB: Vielfalt ist vorteilhaft. So können wir neue Managementstile ausprobieren und auch verschiedene Optionen bei der Entscheidungsfindung ins Auge fassen.

CCP: *Akzeptieren Sie Kritik an Ihrem Führungsstil, ermutigen Sie sogar dazu oder tendieren Sie eher dazu, sie zu vermeiden, allgemein im Führungsteam und generell innerhalb der Belegschaft?*

SB: Entsprechend unserer BASF Strategie schaffen wir Raum für Leistung und persönliche Entwicklung aller Mitarbeiter. In einer solchen Umgebung, die ergänzt wird durch die Feedbackkultur unserer Firma sowie auch durch das bestehende Projekt „Tell me" in unserer Region, kann jeder Mitarbeiter seinem Vorgesetzten oder seinen Kollegen offenes und ehrliches Feedback geben.

CCP: *Wie viele Mitarbeiter hat BASF Zentralasien heute, vor allem in Kasachstan und wie verhält sich diese Anzahl vergleichsweise zur Startperiode von BASF in Kasachstan?*

SB: Gegenwärtig beschäftigen wir in BASF Zentralasien 120 Mitarbeiter, und wir sind in allen großen Städten der Region präsent. Diese Anzahl mag gering erscheinen, jedoch die Einzigartigkeit der Chemieindustrie besteht darin, dass mehrere Jobs in anderen Branchen entstehen, wenn wir auch nur eine neue Arbeitsstelle in unserer Industrie schaffen.

CCP: *Ihre lokalen Mitarbeiter müssen die deutschen Technologien verstehen, die in Kasachstan etabliert sind und die Produkte, die Sie hier herstellen. Sie müssen mit den deutschen Systemen umgehen können. Wie finden Sie Mitarbeiter mit der erforderlichen beruflichen Qualifikation?*

SB: Unsere Firma legt großen Wert auf die Qualifikation der besten lokalen Mitarbeiter, die in der Region verfügbar sind, um das beste Team zu bilden. Wir trainieren und entwickeln sie lokal und in länderübergreifenden Projekten. Dazu kommen Kollegen aus der Zentrale oder wir

schicken unsere Mitarbeiter in die Zentrale; das hängt von der Komplexität einer Technologie oder eines Produkts ab.

CCP: *Werden Sie die BASF Belegschaft in Kasachstan bzw. in Zentralasien erweitern?*

SB: Derzeit sind wir mit unserer Organisationsstruktur gut aufgestellt in der Region. Es hängt alles von den Marktbedingungen ab, wenn jedoch Bedarf an zusätzlichen Arbeitskräften besteht, können wir das tun und, wie ich bereits erwähnt habe, indem wir einen Arbeitsplatz in unserer Branche schaffen, entstehen zwei oder mehr Arbeitsplätze in anderen Branchen.

CCP: *Es gibt eine ganze Reihe von ausländischen Firmen in Kasachstan, sowie in den Nachbarländern, die für die lokale Bevölkerung attraktiv sein können. Wie motivieren Sie Ihre kasachischen Mitarbeiter, bei der BASF zu bleiben, insbesondere in Astana, Almaty und Atyrau?*

SB: Wir bei BASF bilden das beste Team. Wir ziehen die richtigen Leute an und schaffen Voraussetzungen für ihre effektive Arbeit und persönliche Entwicklung. Wir schaffen ein Arbeitsumfeld, das Menschen inspiriert und verbindet und wir praktizieren eine umfassende Führungskultur, die auf gegenseitigem Vertrauen, Respekt und Engagement für maximale Effizienz basiert.

CCP: *Der Umgang mit Mitarbeitern ist ein Aspekt des Managements. Wie Sie mit Kunden interagieren ist ein anderer. Was ist speziell in Bezug auf die Interaktion mit Kunden in Kasachstan, im Vergleich zu Kundenbeziehungsmanagement in Deutschland?*

SB: Ich würde sagen Nähe und Partnerschaftsansatz. Wir behandeln unsere Kunden als enge Partner und tun unser Bestes, um zu ihrem zukünftigen Erfolg beizutragen. Wie bereits erwähnt, arbeiten wir in einem aufstrebenden Markt und agil zu sein und auf die Bedürfnisse unserer Kunden sofort reagieren zu können, das ist ein Schlüssel.

CCP: *Stellen Sie an den Standorten in Kasachstan Produkte für den lokalen Markt her oder auch für den Export in andere asiatische Länder?*

SB: Wir haben zwei Produktionsstandorte in Almaty und Astana für Bauchemikalien, die für das Baugewerbe der Region produzieren, jedoch exportieren wir auch einige Produkte in die Nachbarländer.

CCP: *Sie haben umfangreiche Erfahrungen im Bereich der deutsch-zentral-asiatisch-kasachischen Zusammenarbeit gesammelt. Welchen Rat würden Sie deutschen Managern oder Firmeninhabern geben, die eine Niederlassung in Kasachstan gründen möchten? Ihr Rat könnte ihnen helfen, Fehler zu vermeiden und von Anfang an erfolgreich zu sein.*

SB: Kasachstan ist ein sehr attraktiver und vielversprechender Markt für Investoren, und die lokale Regierung arbeitet ständig an der Verbesserung des Investitionsklimas. Empfehlungen für künftige Investoren? Ich würde sagen, zuerst Market Intelligence und vorbereitende umfassende Arbeit an Fakten und Zahlen. Dann natürlich Verständnis für die lokale Mentalität und Kultur. Und schließlich über den Tellerrand schauen und den deutschen Ansatz mit asiatischer Flexibilität anwenden.

CCP: *Verehrte Frau Baitzhaunova., wir danken Ihnen sehr für dieses interessante Gespräch. Wir sind sicher, dass Ihre Erfahrungen und Erkenntnisse für zukünftige deutsche Investoren und Führungskräfte sehr nützlich sind.*

(Aus dem Englischen übersetzt von S. Mueller)

BASF Central Asia LLP
050016, Rayimbek ave., 211A
Almaty, Kazakhstan

Rashid Kabykayev
Manager corporate communications and government relations
LLP BASF Central Asia,
3A, Charles De Gaulle,
010000 Astana, Kazakhstan
📞 +7 7172 27 04 40-110,
📶 +7 701 029 67 38,
✉ rashid.kabykayev@basf.com

Green Energy 3000 Gruppe projektiert ein 63 MWp-Solarkraftwerk in Südkasachstan

Die Green Energy 3000 Gruppe projektiert seit 2016 in Chulakurgan im südlichen Kasachstan einen Solarpark mit einer solaren Nennleistung von 63 MWp. Der prognostizierte Jahresertrag des Solarkraftwerks von ca. 111 Millionen kWh/Jahr ist so groß, dass damit rechnerisch der Stromverbrauch von 21 625 Einwohnern Kasachstans abgedeckt werden kann. Der durchschnittliche Stromverbrauch pro Einwohner Kasachstans im Jahr 2017 betrug lt. CIA World Factbook – Version Januar 1, 2018 5 133 kWh/Einwohner.

Der *Solarpark* wird sich über eine Fläche von ca. 60 Hektar erstrecken. Direkt am Solarpark wird ein zusätzliches Umspannwerk mit einer Ausgangsspannung von 110 000 Volt errichtet. Es dient der Übertragung der riesigen Leistung in das öffentliche Netz der KEGOC. Der Baubeginn der Anlage wird im vierten Quartal 2018 erfolgen. Die Gesamtbauzeit wird sich über 12 Monate erstrecken.

„Kasachstan in ein sehr attraktives Zielland für Investitionen im Bereich der erneuerbaren Energien", betont Andreas Renker, Geschäftsführer der Green Energy 3000 Holding GmbH mit Sitz in Leipzig. „Der WTO-Beitritt 2015, politische Stabilität, klare und investitionsfördernde Strukturen sowie gesetzliche Regelungen im Bereich der Förderung Erneuerbarer Energien und ideale klimatische und Witterungsbedingungen für Wind- und Solarkraftanlagen sind für uns Gründe genug, uns in diesem Land zu engagieren", ergänzt Renker.

Erste Schritte in dem zentralasiatischen Land hat Green Energy 3000 bereits Anfang 2016 unternommen. Mittlerweile verfügt die Firmengruppe über eine Niederlassung in Almaty sowie mehrere ortsansässige Zweckgesellschaften für die Umsetzung von Projekten im Bereich der Erneuerbaren Energien. Darüber hinaus wurden Anteile an einer Baufirma erworben, welche das Know-How sowie die Zulassungen besitzt, die bauliche Realisierung der Projekte umzusetzen. Für den Herbst 2018 plant Green Energy 3000 die Teilnahme an der Ausschreibung für weitere Erneuerbare Energien-Projekte in Kasachstan.

Green Energy 3000 ist ein erfahrener internationaler Projektentwickler und Generalunternehmer im Bereich der Erneuerbaren Energien. Seit 2004 besitzt Green Energy 3000 umfangreiches Know-How von der

Standortakquise und Projektplanung bis hin zu internationalem Komponenteneinkauf, Finanzierung und Errichtung von Solar- und Windkraftanlagen. Darüber hinaus begleitet Green Energy 3000 die fertigen Anlagen international durch technische und kaufmännische Betriebsführung (Operation & Management; O&M).

Als neues Geschäftsfeld engagiert sich Green Energy 3000 seit 2017 im Bereich der Energiespeicherung und ermöglicht damit nicht nur produzierenden Unternehmen, ihre Stromkosten zu senken, sondern trägt durch Lastspitzenkappung und Netzentlastung aktiv dazu bei, den weiteren Ausbau der Erneuerbaren Energien möglich zu machen. Insgesamt 50 Mitarbeiter in Deutschland, Frankreich und Kasachstan tragen zum Erfolg der Firmengruppe bei.

Green Energy 3000 GmbH
Torgauer Straße 231
04347 Leipzig, Germany
📞 +49 (0)341 35 56 04 0
✉ info@ge3000.de
🌐 www.ge3000.de

TOO Green Energy 3000 Kazakhstan
Mukanov Str., 113
Business Center "Rich"
050026 Almaty, Republic of Kazakstan

Kasachstan bietet für Erneuerbare Energien äußerst attraktive Rahmenbedingungen

Interview mit
Herrn Dipl.-Ing. Andreas Renker,
Geschäftsführer, Green Energy 3000
Holding GmbH, Leipzig

CCP: *Herr Renker, Ihre Firma heißt Green Energy 3000. Was bedeutet die 3000?*

AR: Durch die 3000 drückt sich in Kombination mit der Bezugnahme auf grüne Energie der Gedanke der Nachhaltigkeit in all ihren Facetten aus. In diesem Sinne steht die 3000 für Zukunft und unerschöpfliche erneuerbare Energie. Dinge, für die unser Unternehmen seit seiner Gründung einsteht.

CCP: *Seit 2016 sind Sie in Kasachstan tätig, in einem äußerst wichtigen Wirtschaftszweig, im Bereich Erneuerbarer Energie. Produziert das Land jetzt bereits einen Teil des nationalen Energieaufkommens aus diesem Bereich oder bisher nur aus fossilen Rohstoffen, wie die Karaganda Steinkohle?*

AR: Kasachstan unternimmt enorme Anstrengungen, mittelfristig einen großen Teil seines Energiebedarfs aus erneuerbaren Energiequellen zu decken. Es gibt hier ein sehr großes Potential, das aktuell jedoch noch kaum ausgeschöpft wird. Dies wird sich jedoch in den nächsten Jahren dramatisch ändern.

CCP: *Welche Kriterien haben Ihre Firma zur Entscheidung für Kasachstan als Investmentdestination veranlasst?*

AR: Kasachstan bietet für Erneuerbare Energien äußerst attraktive Rahmenbedingungen. Die Grundlage bilden die klimatischen Bedingungen, welche durch attraktive Windregionen und insbesondere im Süden durch eine starke Sonneneinstrahlung gekennzeichnet sind. Hier produzieren Photovoltaikanlagen pro installierter kWp Leistung ganz andere Energiemengen pro Jahr als etwa in Deutschland. Die investitionsfördernden Strukturen und gesetzlichen Regelungen im Bereich der Förderung erneuerbarer Energien ermöglichen auf dieser Basis, in erneuerbare Energien zu investieren. Nicht zuletzt der WTO-Beitritt 2015 und eine recht hohe politische Stabilität kommen dazu.

CCP: *Wie ist Ihre Firma in Kasachstan vertreten: mit einer Repräsentanz oder durch Händler oder produzieren Sie dort bereits?*

AR: Wir sind durch eine Repräsentanz vertreten, welche eng mit unseren Projektmanagern an unserem Hauptsitz in Leipzig zusammenarbeitet. So verzahnen wir unser internationales und interdisziplinäres Team am Stammsitz mit unserem Projektmanagement und lokaler Expertise vor Ort.

CCP: *Welche Art Erneuerbarer Energie haben Sie vor, in Kasachstan am stärksten zu entwickeln?*

AR: Aktuell sind unsere Schwerpunkte Photovoltaik und Windenergie. Für unsere 63 MWp-Photovoltaikanlage in Chulakkurgan wird der Baubeginn noch 2018 stattfinden. Weitere Projekte, zu denen auch Windparks gehören, bereiten wir aktuell konkret vor. Weitere Bereiche wie etwa Biogas bieten mittelfristig ebenfalls interessante Möglichkeiten.

CCP: *Kasachstan hat lange Winter mit viel Schnee und Sturm, was wird aus Ihren Solaranlagen in dieser Jahreszeit?*

AR: Chulakkurgan liegt in einer Steppenregion und ist durch kontinentales Klima gekennzeichnet. Dort sind Niederschläge, die sich negativ auf den Ertrag unserer Anlage auswirken, relativ selten. Dazu kommen aufgrund der südlichen Lage über das Jahr hinweg hohe Einstrahlungswerte, die auch im Winter noch recht hoch, wenngleich natürlich deutlich niedriger als im Sommer sind. Dies ist jedoch bei Solaranlagen fast überall so.

CCP: *Kasachstan hat unendlich große Steppenflächen ebenso wie bis zu 7000m Gebirgshöhe. Denken Sie daran, Windparks anzulegen?*

AR: Windparks zählen ebenfalls zu unseren Investitionsvorhaben in Kasachstan. Es gibt viele attraktive Windregionen mit hohen durchschnittlichen Windgeschwindigkeiten, etwa im Norden des Landes.

CCP: *Das Klima ist mit unvorhersehbaren Schwankungen und sogar Unwettern verbunden, die Ausfälle und also Verluste in der Energieerzeugung aus Sonne und / oder Wind verursachen. Ist es nicht sicherer, Erneuerbare Energie aus den Bio-Abfällen der starken kasachischen Landwirtschaft zu entwickeln?*

AR: Dies ist eine gute Ergänzung zu den beschriebenen Energiequellen, da Biomasse weniger wetterabhängig ist. Die Energiewende erfordert jedoch die Nutzbarmachung verschiedener Energiequellen.

CCP: *Green Energy 3000 ist bestimmt nicht allein im kasachischen Markt. Vermutlich sind Kanadier und Amerikaner auch in Ihrem Bereich aktiv. Was zeichnet Ihre Anlagen gegenüber jenen aus?*

AR: Investoren aus verschiedenen Ländern engagieren sich in Kasachstan, nicht zuletzt auch in den neu geschaffenen Ausschreibungen. Unser Anspruch ist es, uns mit deutscher Ingenieurskunst auf diesem Markt zu etablieren und in den verbauten Komponenten die bestmögliche Qualität zu realisieren. So können wir sicherstellen, dass die Anlagen die geforderte Laufzeit ohne Einschränkungen laufen und gleichzeitig den neuesten Stand der Technik verwenden.

CCP: *Welche Ziele haben Sie sich gesetzt für die Entwicklung Ihrer Firma im kasachischen Markt für die nächsten fünf Jahre und im Rahmen der Entwicklung Kasachstans bis 2050?*

AR: Wir möchten uns mit der Realisierung mehrerer Projekte weiter im kasachischen Markt etablieren und im Rahmen des neu geschaffenen Ausschreibungsmodells erfolgreich sein. Perspektivisch würde es uns dabei natürlich freuen, tragender Teil der Energiewende in Kasachstan zu sein und als wichtiger Akteur dazu beizutragen, die großen Potentiale des Landes im Bereich Erneuerbarer Energien nutzbar zu machen.

CCP: *Arbeiten Sie mit kasachischen Energie-Experten zusammen?*

AR: Eine enge Zusammenarbeit mit lokalen und regionalen Experten ist für jedes Erneuerbare Energien-Projekt essentiell. In Kasachstan ist die Zusammenarbeit mit kasachischen Experten etwa im Rahmen der notwendigen Expertise und für die Erlangung der Baugenehmigung wichtig. Wir freuen uns, unsere regionale Expertise dabei noch weiter ausbauen zu können.

CCP: *In welcher Sprache operieren Sie in Kasachstan?*

AR: In unserem internationalen Team ist über das Deutsche und Französische hinaus die kasachische und russische und je nach Gegebenheit die englische Sprache zu hören.

CCP: *Wie war die Zusammenarbeit mit den staatlichen Verwaltungen in Kasachstan in der Startperiode Ihrer Firma?*

AR: Wir haben ein wohlwollendes Klima vorgefunden und konnten unsere Themen jederzeit adressieren. Wir können uns nicht beklagen.

CCP: *Welche Erfahrungen in der deutsch-kasachischen Zusammenarbeit möchten Sie an deutsche Exekutives bzw. Firmeninhaber weitergeben, die nach Ihnen nach Kasachstan kommen?*

AR: Ein zentraler Erfolgsfaktor ist, selbstverständlich neben dem ansonsten stimmigen Geschäftsmodell für den Markteintritt, die Kenntnis der lokalen und regionalen Spezifika. Wer sich vor Ort sprachlich und kulturell souverän bewegen kann, hat vor Ort bessere Erfolgschancen.

CCP: *Vielen Dank, sehr geehrter Herr Renker, für Ihre interessanten Statements. Sicherlich sind sie hilfreich für künftige deutsche Investoren in Kasachstan.*

Green Energy 3000 GmbH
Torgauer Straße 231
DE-04347 Leipzig
☎ +49 (0)341 35 56 04 0
✉ info@ge3000.de
🌐 www.ge3000.de

TOO Green Energy 3000 Kazakhstan
Mukanov Str., 113
Business Center "Rich"
050026 Almaty Republic of Kazakhstan

Brücke Europa-Asien:

LORENZ Handels GmbH, Neuhof, Germany

und

Managing Company Shanyrak GmbH, Astana, Kasachstan

General Manager:
Alexander Lorenz
📞 +7 (7172) 55 28 54
📱 +7 701 888 87 71
✉ a.lorenz@shanyrak-group.kz
🌐 www.shanyrak-group.kz

Die Shanyrak Gruppe

- **Capital Projects Ltd.**
  Herstellung von Mischfutter und Hühnerfleisch, 600 Arbeitsplätze
- **Agrointerptiza GmbH**
  Herstellung von kommerziellen Eiern, 230 Arbeitsplätze
- **Geflügelfarm Namens K. Marx GmbH**
  Herstellung von kommerziellen Eiern, 220 Arbeitsplätze
- **Geflügelfarm Tselinogradskaja GmbH**
  Herstellung von kommerziellen Eiern, 85 Arbeitsplätze
- **Plemptizetorg GmbH**
  Herstellung von Bruteiern, 60 Arbeitsplätze
- **Energia-Kapital GmbH**
  Herstellung von Backwaren
- **JSC Akmola – Feniks AG, Akmola-Feniks Plus**
  TOO Shanyrak Agro: Pflanzenproduktion,
  38 000 ha, 335 Arbeitsplätze, Futtermittelproduktion
- **Eco Pack Astana GmbH**
  Herstellung von Eierverpackungen, 21 Arbeitsplätze
- **Bio-Katu Ltd.:** Herstellung von organischem Bio-Dünger

LORENZ Handels GmbH, Neuhof, Germany und Managing Company Shanyrak Ltd., Astana, Kasachstan

Eine Brücke zwischen Europa und Asien bildet die LORENZ Handels GmbH in Neuhof, in Deutschland, nach Asien, denn sie ist die Einkaufsorganisation für die Shanyrak Gruppe in Kasachstan.

Alexander Lorenz stattet seine Unternehmen in Kasachstan mit den modernsten Maschinen aus Europa aus: aus Deutschland, Belgien, Holland und der Schweiz.

Die Managing Company Shanyrak GmbH hat ihren Sitz in der kasachischen Hauptstadt Astana, leitet von hier aus eine Gruppe von 11 landwirtschaftlichen Unternehmen, angesiedelt an verschiedenen Orten im Westen Kasachstans – von Kokshetau, im Gebiet Akmola, im Norden, über Karaganda bis Almaty im Süden. Sie beschäftigt 1 800 Mitarbeiter und befindet sich ständig im Wachstum.

Auf der Basis von 38 000 ha landwirtschaftlicher Fläche, wo die Gruppe jährlich 40 000 Tonnen Futtermittel für fünf Farmen produziert, führt die Gruppe auch eine Brotfabrik. Außerdem stellt sie selbst die Verpackungen für Eier her, aus Altpapier, das in den Städten gesammelt wird.

Die Managing Company Shanyrak GmbH produzierte im Jahr 2017 360 Mio. Eier für den Export nach Russland, Afghanistan, Tadschikistan und erweitert künftig den Export in den Iran. Außerdem produziert die Gruppe 20 000 Tonnen Hähnchen-Schlachtgut pro Jahr und beliefert täglich 500 Geschäfte in Astana und im Umland mit Hühnerfleisch.

Die Managing Company Shanyrak GmbH strebt an, eine komplett selbständige Wertschöpfungskette zu werden.

Managing Company Shanyrak GmbH
Alexander Lorenz
General Manager
Akmola Region, Tselinograd Bezirk,
Dorf Akmol, Str. Gagarina 14
021800, Republik Kasachstan
📞 +7 772 55 28 54
📶 +7 701 886 87 71
✉ a.lorenz@shanyrak-group.kz
🌐 www.shanyrak-group.kz

Erfolg in Kasachstan.
Die Lorenz Strategie: Klein beginnen, aktiv sein und korrekt arbeiten, mit ersten Erfolgen Vertrauen aufbauen und dann wachsen

Interview mit Herrn Alexander Lorenz, General Manager der Managing Company Shanyrak GmbH, Astana

CCP: *Herr Lorenz, wir danken Ihnen im Voraus für Ihre Bereitschaft zu diesem Interview, denn als General Manager von einem Netz von ca. 11 Teilunternehmen ist Ihre Agenda täglich übervoll von Terminen. Lassen Sie bitte die Leser dieses Buches ein wenig Einblick nehmen in Ihren Lebenslauf. Sie haben einen deutschen Familiennamen und russischen Vornamen. Wann sind Ihre Ur- oder Ur-ur-Großeltern nach Kasachstan ausgewandert und aus welchem Grund?*

AL: Meine Vorfahren stammen aus Baunatal bei Kassel. Sie waren Bauern und sind dem Aufruf der Kaiserin Katharina II. von 1763 gefolgt, sich an der Wolga anzusiedeln, in dem autonomen Gebiet, das ihnen zugesagt wurde. Sie führten dort Landwirtschaft und bauten vor allem Weizen an. In der Stalinzeit, vor dem 2. Weltkrieg, wurden sie gewaltsam umgesiedelt, weit in den Osten der damaligen Sowjetunion, nach Kasachstan. Dort mussten sie in einer Kolchose arbeiten. Mein Vater war damals sechs Jahre alt.

CCP: *Sie sind also in Kasachstan geboren, als Sohn der Eltern von Kolchosbauern und aufgewachsen im Gebiet Karaganda, wo Sie auch in die Schule gegangen sind.*

AL: Ja, ganz richtig. So war es.

CCP: *Wo haben Sie dann Ihre berufliche Ausbildung erhalten und welche?*

AL: Ich habe zuerst eine Ausbildung in Astana (damals Zelinograd) abgeschlossen, studierte danach an der Universität von Arkalyk und später an der Ost-Kasachstan-Universität in Ust-Kaminogorsk. Auf diesem Wege habe ich kaufmännische und wirtschaftliche Berufe erlernt.

CCP: *Sie verfügen heute über ein unermessliches Managementwissen und -können. Wie verlief Ihre berufliche Laufbahn?*

AL: Nach meiner Ausbildung arbeitete ich zehn Jahre in verschiedenen Betrieben in Arkalyk, danach dreizehn Jahre als Stellvertretender Direktor in Ost-Kasachstan. In Arkalyk habe ich im Jahr 1973 Tatjana geheiratet und dort wurden zwei Kinder geboren: im Jahr 1974 – Tochter Viktoria, und im Jahr 1978 – Sohn Alexej. Meine Eltern waren inzwischen nach Deutschland zurückgegangen und ich folgte ihnen mit meiner Familie im Jahr 1996. Zuerst lernte ich intensiv Deutsch und dann gründete ich meine erste Firma in Neuhof. Ich verkaufte deutsche Anlagen für Hühnerfarmen und Hähnchenmast nach Russland und Kasachstan.

CCP: *Diese Firma in Neuhof leitet heute Ihre Frau Tatjana Lorenz, und Sie gründeten zahlreiche weitere Firmen in Kasachstan. Das scheint leicht zu sein. Was können Sie einem deutschen mittelständischen Unternehmer empfehlen zu tun, damit er ebenso erfolgreich gründet in Kasachstan wie Sie?*

AL: Arbeit gibt es genug in Kasachstan. Man muss einfach wissen, was man will, kommen, sich umsehen und Kontakt aufnehmen, zuerst mit der Stadtverwaltung. Es gibt viele Möglichkeiten, Zuschüsse und Hilfe jeder Art zu bekommen. Die Nachfrage an Investoren in Kasachstan ist hoch. Allerdings muss man auch viel Geduld mitbringen und selbst sehr aktiv sein.

CCP: *Ist die Landwirtschaft Ihrer Meinung nach der Bereich, wo deutsche Mittelständer die größten Chancen haben zur Modernisierung beizutragen?*

AL: Ja, unbedingt. Unterstützung wird gewiss gegeben, man muss nur die entsprechenden Anträge an den Staat stellen. Dabei hilft auch der deutsch-kasachische Verein *Wiedergeburt*.

CCP: *Das ist ja sehr erfreulich. Nennen Sie doch bitte einige Tätigkeitsfelder, wo das Know-how des deutschen Mittelstandes in Kasachstan sehr gefragt und notwendig ist.*

AL: Deutsche werden in Kasachstan überall geschätzt. Dieses positive Image verdanken wir der guten Arbeit unserer Vorfahren. Gut, ehrlich und vertrauenswürdig, das sind die Standards, die man Deutschen zuschreibt, und die man erwartet. Dieses Bild vom Deutschen ist bereits in der Kolchose entstanden – durch gute Arbeit. Sie haben viel geschafft.

CCP: *Das ist wahr – und Sie haben auch viel geschafft. Sie brauchen viele verschiedene Fachkräfte für Ihre verschiedenen Firmen – für den Umgang mit modernen monitorgesteuerten Landwirtschaftsmaschinen und Prozessanlagen aus Deutschland, der Schweiz und Belgien, für wissenschaftlich begründeten Futtermittelanbau, für effektive Eier- und Fleischproduktion, 24-Stunden-laufende Logistik und mehr. Wo finden Sie die zahlreichen Fachkräfte?*

AL: Wir laden Experten aus verschiedenen Ländern ein, aus Deutschland, Holland und anderen europäischen Ländern zur Ausbildung. Wir bieten theoretische Ausbildung, verbunden mit praktischer Anwendung. So gewinnen wir gute Fachkräfte.

CCP: *Leben und arbeiten auf dem Lande in Kasachstan ist wahrscheinlich nicht so komfortabel wie das Leben in Astana. Wie motivieren Sie Ihre Mitarbeiter, in Ihren Firmen zu arbeiten und zu bleiben?*

AL: Auf dem Lande gab es zuerst gar keine Arbeit, egal wo. Dann haben wir zum Beispiel in Akmola die moderne Hühnerfarm aufgebaut, mit dem allerhöchsten Lohnniveau im Gebiet Akmola. Außerdem bekommen unsere Mitarbeiter kostenlose Arbeitskleidung, Komfort am Arbeitsplatz, wie Wasch-, Dusch-, Umkleide- und Speiseräume, kostenlose Verpflegung, sowie Sozialversicherung. Jetzt kommen die Leute von selbst aus der Stadt ins Dorf zurück und möchten bei uns arbeiten.

CCP: *Welche Empfehlungen geben Sie einem deutschen Firmenleiter für den Umgang mit kasachischem Personal, damit die Zusammenarbeit erfolgreich verläuft?*

AL: Freundlich sein und ehrlich, Verständnis aufbringen und nicht überheblich auftreten. Natürlich sollte man die Sprache der Mitarbeiter sprechen.

CCP: *Wenn Schwierigkeiten im Produktionsprozess auftreten, seien es Energie-, Wasser-, Gebäude- oder andere Probleme, wer sind die lokalen Partner, die helfen?*

AL: Die Leute vor Ort, in der Stadt- bzw. Gebietsverwaltung, helfen gern, man muss nur seine Probleme darlegen und mit ihnen zusammen nach Lösungen suchen.

CCP: *In Kasachstan gibt es zurzeit keine deutsche Bank; deutsche Firmen müssen also vor Ort mit kasachischen Banken zusammenarbeiten. Sie haben große Erfahrung auf diesem Gebiet. Können Sie einem deutschen mittelständischen Unternehmer, der in Deutschland keinen Kredit bekommt, so unterstützen, dass er in Kasachstan Finanzierung für Unternehmenswachstum bekommt?*

AL: Kommt auf sein Projekt an, jede Bank braucht Garantie, zum Beispiel Gebäude oder dergleichen. Man muss nicht am Anfang alles wollen, sondern klein anfangen, bescheiden sein und fleißig, zeigen, was man kann, mit ersten Erfolgen Vertrauen aufbauen und dann organisch Schritt für Schritt wachsen. In der Müllverarbeitung zum Beispiel mit einer Maschine beginnen, positiven Effekt zeigen gegenüber der Bank, dann wird man bestimmt weitere Unterstützung bekommen.

CCP: *Sie sind heute 65 Jahre, sind der Kopf einer sehr erfolgreichen Unternehmensgruppe, erhielten zahlreiche staatliche Auszeichnungen und haben noch immer Zukunftsziele, welche?*

AL: Als erstes habe ich vorn die bestehenden Hühnerfarmen um eine Düngerproduktion und Fleischproduktion zu erweitern. Des Weiteren planen wir eine Fabrik zur Verarbeitung von Eiern in Eipulver zu errichten, die den weltweiten Standards entspricht, die Bedürfnisse Kasachstans deckt sowie auch für den Export arbeitet.

CCP: *Das sind große Pläne, Herr Lorenz. Wir wünschen Ihnen jedenfalls weiterhin viel Erfolg in Ihren gegenwärtigen und ebenso viel Erfolg in Ihren künftigen Unternehmungen.*

Managing Company Shanyrak GmbH
Alexander Lorenz
General Manager
Akmola Region, Tselinograd Bezirk,
Dorf Akmol, Str. Gagarina 14
021800, Republik Kasachstan
📞 +7 772 55 28 54
📱 +7 701 886 87 71
✉ a.lorenz@shanyrak-group.kz
🌐 www.shanyrak-group.kz

Amazonen-Werke
H. Dreyer GmbH & Co.KG

Die Amazonen-Werke mit Hauptsitz in Hasbergen-Gaste, unweit von Osnabrück, stellen Land- und Kommunalmaschinen her. Das inhabergeführte Unternehmen der Familie Dreyer beschäftigt an sieben verschiedenen Produktionsstandorten in Deutschland, Frankreich, Russland und Ungarn rund 1 850 Mitarbeiter.

Zum Produktionsprogramm zählen Bodenbearbeitungsmaschinen, Sämaschinen, Düngerstreuer und Pflanzenschutzspritzen. Auf Basis dieser Kernkompetenzen ist Amazone heute der Spezialist für den Intelligenten Pflanzenbau in der Landwirtschaft. Außerdem produziert Amazone Maschinen für die Park- und Grünflächenpflege sowie den Winterdienst. Bei seinen Kunden genießt Amazone dank hervorragender Qualität sowie innovativen Produkten einen sehr guten Ruf.

2017 hat Amazone Maschinen im Wert von rund 457 Mio. € verkauft. Da sich Amazone im Laufe seiner über 135-jährigen Geschichte zu einem global tätigen Systemanbieter entwickelt hat, werden heute rund 80 Prozent der Produktion in über 70 Länder verkauft.

Um dieser Tendenz gerecht zu werden und in den Zielmärkten in Asien die erforderliche Präsenz zu zeigen, beschloss die Geschäftsleitung in 2010, in Kasachstans Hauptstadt Astana eine Niederlassung zu gründen, die Amazone TOO. Durch diesen Schritt konnte die vor Ort notwendige Qualität im Bereich Verkaufsberatung und After Sales Service entwickelt werden. Kasachstan ist mit etwa 20 Mio. Hektar Ackerfläche ein wichtiger Markt für die Amazone-Werke. Um den Anforderungen unserer Kunden gerecht zu werden, haben wir neben der Zentrale in Astana weitere Standorte im Landwirtschaftsgebiet im Norden, in *Kustanai* und *Kokschetau* eröffnet.

In Kokschetau wurde darüber hinaus ein umfangreiches Ersatzteillager aufgebaut, um möglichst jederzeit in der Saison die Maschinen optimal betreuen zu können. Ein Großteil der kasachischen Mitarbeiter wird jährlich im Stammwerk in Deutschland geschult. Dies ist absolut notwendig, da auf den Feldern Kasachstans die modernsten und innovativsten Maschinen von Amazone arbeiten.

Darüber hinaus ist die Amazone TOO Astana aktiv in der Neu- und Weiterentwicklung von Amazone-Maschinen beteiligt. So werden in

Zusammenarbeit mit deutschen und kasachischen Forschungseinrichtungen Maschinen für die spezifischen Anforderungen in Nordkasachstan entwickelt und getestet. Dies geschieht auch durch die Unterstützung des Bundesministeriums für Bildung und Forschung in Form des Projektes „Rekks".

AMAZONE TOO
Republik Kasachstan,
Astana 010000, Rayon Saryarka
Saifullina-Straße 3, Haus 3, Büro 1
📞 +7 705 29 51 88 6,
📶 +49 151 17 11 77 01
✉ Dr.Tobias.Meinel@amazone.de

ТОО «АМАЗОНЕ»
Республика Казахстан,
010000, город Астана, район Сарыарка
ул. Сейфуллина д. 3,НП-1
📞 +7 717 23 47 9 49, +7 701 52 40 914
✉ dr.Tobias.Meinel@amazone.de
   Oxana.Privalenko@amazone.kz

AMAZONEN-WERKE H. Dreyer GmbH & Co. KG
Am Amazonenwerk 9-13
D-49205 Hasbergen, Germany
📞 +49 (0)5405 501-0
✉ amazone@amazone.de
🌐 www.amazone.de

Amazone: Agronomische und technische Lösungen für nachhaltigen Pflanzenbau in den eurasischen Steppen

Interview mit Herrn
Dr. rer. nat. Tobias Meinel,
General Director, TOO Amazone,
Astana, Kasachstan

CCP: *Herr Dr. Meinel, Amazone ist heute im Weltmarkt ein Spezialist für intelligenten Pflanzenbau in der Landwirtschaft und mit diesem Profil startete Ihre Firma in 2010 den Verkauf modernster Landtechnik. Sie leiten nunmehr seit acht Jahren die Verkaufsberatung und den After Sales Service. Wie viele Mitarbeiter haben Sie?*

TM: In unserer Geschäftsstelle hier in Astana sind 12 kasachische Mitarbeiter tätig, die durch unsere Schulungen die Qualifikation haben, unsere Maschinen vor Ort optimal zu betreuen.

CCP: *Uns interessiert der Beitrag von Amazone zur Modernisierung der Landwirtschaft in Kasachstan. Um das zu erkennen, beschreiben Sie doch bitte den Stand der Landtechnik, den Sie im Startjahr 2010 hier vorgefunden haben.*

TM: Um es kurz zu sagen, wir fanden oftmals die Landtechnik auf einem Niveau von 1975 vor. Das bedeutet: die Landwirte brachten die Saat mit veralteten Sämaschinen aus, ohne Dünger und ohne Pflanzenschutzmittel.

CCP: *Sollte man nicht annehmen können, dass junge kasachische Agronomen von den hiesigen Universitäten schon lange „frischen Wind" in die Landwirtschaft ihres Landes gebracht haben?*

TB: „Frischer Wind" kommt wie überall in der Welt auch in Kasachstan besonders von den Absolventen der Universitäten. Die Jugend hier ist hochmotiviert und leistungsbereit. Der Nachwuchs will den Fortschritt, ist wissbegierig und fordert manche Lehrkräfte damit sicherlich oft sehr heraus. Die jungen Akademiker wollen modernste Produktionsmethoden studieren und den landtechnischen Fortschritt nutzen. Wichtig ist, dass diesen jungen Agronomen dann auch Perspektiven in der Landwirtschaft vor Ort geboten werden und nicht nur in der Hauptstadt Astana.

CCP: *Das heißt, Sie müssen mit dem Verkauf der modernen Amazone Landtechnik auch Fortbildung anbieten. Sie betreuen ein Landwirtschaftsgebiet im Norden und Nordwesten mit einem Aktionsradius von 700 x 1000 km. Wie viele Leute haben Sie in diesem Raum in acht Jahren fit gemacht für die Bedienung Ihrer modernen Maschinen?*

TM: Sicherlich über 700. Das sind unsere Assets: Ausbildung theoretisch, praktisch an der Maschine selbst in der Farm sowie im Einsatz auf dem Feld und 24 Stunden Servicebereitschaft. Zur Realisierung und Unterstützung dieses Services unterhalten wir ein sehr umfangreiches Ersatzteillager in Kokschetau. Innerhalb von 24 Stunden können wir Ersatzteile bis in das entfernteste Dorf in Kasachstan liefern. Falls doch ein notwendiges Ersatzteil nicht am Lager ist, können wir es innerhalb von drei Tagen aus Deutschland bereitstellen.

CCP: *Ausbildung erfordert Sprache, Herr Dr. Meinel, Sie sprechen also perfekt Russisch?*

TM: Ja, ich habe in Barnaul, in Russland, studiert. Russich sprechen können hilft mir unter anderem bei meiner Tätigkeit in Kasachstan.

CCP: *Beschreiben Sie doch bitte die moderne Technik etwas näher, die Sie hier in der kasachischen Landwirtschaft einführen.*

TM: Das mache ich gern. Es geht grundsätzlich um agronomische und technische Lösungen für einen nachhaltigen Pflanzenbau in den eurasischen Steppen, mit anderen Worten, um ressourcenschonende Landwirtschaft und Einführung innovativer klimaangepasster Landtechnik. Ein Teil davon ist die Großflächensätechnik. Ein Feld hat eine Dimension von ca. 2 x 2 Kilometer! Unsere Amazone Sämaschine ist 15 m breit sät und bringt gleichzeitig Dünger aus. Unsere Pflanzenschutzspritzen sind satellitengesteuert. Der Traktor wird so gesteuert, dass keine Fläche unbearbeitet bleibt und der Traktorist kann seinen Arbeitsverlauf an einem Bildschirm genau verfolgen.

CCP: *Pflanzenschutzmittel, das sind wahrscheinlich Schutzmittel gegen Befall mit Ungeziefer, sogenannte Pestizide, richtig?*

TM: Ja, zum Teil. Besonders wichtig ist die passgenaue Ausbringung von Herbiziden, die die konkurrierenden Unkräuter bekämpfen.

CCP: *Auf den riesigen Flächen fallen dabei sicher immense Kosten an, und das kann ja auch ökologisch bedenklich sein. Hat Amazone dafür eine agronomisch-technische Lösung?*

TM: Ja, diese Lösung heißt *UX AmaSpot.* Amazone ist weltweit die einzige Firma, die eine solche Maschine herstellt. Die Gestänge der Maschine sind mit Sensoren ausgerüstet, die Unkraut erkennen, das punktweise wächst und daher auch punktweise vernichtet werden kann, anstatt das ganze Feld unnötig mit dem chemischen Unkrautvernichtungsmittel zu besprühen. So werden Boden und Kulturpflanzen gleichzeitig geschont und immens Kosten gespart

CCP: *Das hört sich großartig an, Herr Dr. Meinel, und ermöglicht der kasachischen Landwirtschaft große Erträge. Jedoch, können die Farmen diese Maschinen auch alle kaufen?*

TM: Mit dieser Frage berühren Sie einen wunden Punkt. Die Bauern möchten diese Maschinen sehr gern kaufen, allerdings stoßen sie dabei auf ein Problem, das vorher auf politischer Ebene gelöst werden müsste. In Kasachstan sind die Kredite sehr teuer. Die deutschen Banken gewähren Kredite nur mit einer Laufzeit von sechs Monaten, weil Hermes im Augenblick auch nur für sechs Monate versichert. Der Landwirt braucht jedoch, wie in anderen Ländern, eine Kreditlaufzeit von mindestens drei Jahren, damit er die Investition mit drei verkauften Ernten gut finanzieren kann.

CCP: *Da können wir nur hoffen, Herr Dr. Meinel, dass dieses Problem bekannt genug ist und an der Lösung bereits gearbeitet wird. Welche Ziele stellt sich Amazone für die Zukunft?*

TM: Weiterhin exzellente pflanzenbauliche Beratung bieten, mehr von unseren Maschinen verkaufen, Nachhaltigkeit ohne Bodenzerstörung in Kasachstan fördern, Vertiefung der Verkaufsberatung, Aufrechterhaltung und Intensivierung des Tag-und-Nacht-Services und so umfassende Kundenzufriedenheit gewähren und behalten. Das sind unsere Ziele.

CCP: *Wir wünschen Ihnen, dass Sie sie erreichen. Bevor wir uns verabschieden jedoch noch eine zukunftsträchtige Frage: Welche Botschaft möchten Sie an künftige deutsche Exekutives vermitteln, die nach Kasachstan kommen werden?*

TM: Die einheimischen Sprachen und Traditionen zu kennen ist ein Vorteil, denn dadurch entsteht das notwendige persönliche

Vertrauensverhältnis, das für gute Zusammenarbeit unerlässlich ist. Weiterhin braucht man viel Geduld, denn die Republik ist noch jung und auf dem Land geht die Entwicklung manchmal nicht so schnell wie in der Stadt. Jedoch kann ich nur empfehlen, nach Kasachstan zu kommen. Es macht große Freude mit den Menschen hier zu lernen, zu arbeiten und zu leben. Nicht ohne Grund bin ich schon acht Jahre hier.

CCP: *Vielen Dank für das sehr interessante Gespräch.*

AMAZONE TOO
Republik Kasachstan,
Astana 010000, Rayon Saryarka
Saifullina-Straße 3, Haus 3, Büro 1
📞 +7 705 29 51 88 6,
📡 +49 151 17 11 77 01
✉ Dr.Tobias.Meinel@amazone.de

ТОО «АМАЗОНЕ»
Республика Казахстан,
010000, город Астана, район Сарыарка
ул. Сейфуллина д. 3,НП-1
📞 +7 717 23 47 9 49, +7 701 52 40 914
✉ Dr.Tobias.Meinel@amazone.de
   Oxana.Privalenko@amazone.kz

AMAZONEN-WERKE H. Dreyer GmbH & Co. KG
Am Amazonenwerk 9-13
D-49205 Hasbergen, Germany
📞 +49 (0)5405 501-0
✉ amazone@amazone.de
🌐 www.amazone.de

Anlage für Rohrisolierung Isoplus Central Asia LLP

Die Anlage für Rohrisolierung Isoplus Zentralasien LLP ist eine Tochtergesellschaft der europäischen Unternehmensgruppe Isoplus. Sie produziert in Kasachstan und liefert vorgedämmte Rohrsysteme für Fernwärmeleitungen und Produktionsstätten verschiedener Arten.

Die Anlage wurde im Jahre 2014 vom Präsidenten Nursultan Nasarbayev eröffnet, und zwar durch Übernahme der gesamten Produktionstechnologie von der Muttergesellschaft Isoplus Central Asia LLP. So wurde in Kasachstan deutsche Qualität in der Herstellung von vorgedämmten Rohrsystemen und Formstücken etabliert. Mit qualitativ hochwertigen Materialien und neuen Technologien erreichen wir Bestleistungen in wichtigen Parametern wie:

- Wärmeleitfähigkeit,
- Qualität der Isolierung,
- Qualität der Isolierung von Rohrverbindungen,
- Lebensdauer von vorisolierten Wärmenetzen,
- Optimierung von Rohrleitungssperren.

Isoplus Zentralasien LLP ist der erste Hersteller in den GUS-Staaten, der ein wärmeisolierendes Material auf der Grundlage von Cyclopentan mit einem Koeffizienten thermischer Leitfähigkeit von 0,0275 W/(m*K) herstellt und anwendet.

Isoplus nutzt ein 2-Komponenten-System (Polyol und Isocyanat) von BASF und als Treibmittel Cyclopentan. Während der exothermischen und chemischen Reaktionen wird ein qualitativ hochwertiges hartes Isolationsmaterial hergestellt, mit einer verbesserten Wärmeleitfähigkeit von 0,0275 W/(m*K), EN 253. Dies führt zu einer Reduzierung der Wärmeverluste in Fernwärmenetzen von ca. 30 Prozent, im Vergleich zu dem traditionell verwendeten Dämmstoff, der auf der Basis CO_2 und Freon funktioniert.

Isopus Central Asia LLP ist der führende Hersteller von vorgedämmten Rohrsystemen in Kasachstan. Hier einige Kennziffern:
- Anzahl der Beschäftigten: 150.
- Produktionskapazität 2017: DN1000-100km/Jahr, DN500 1km/Tag.
- Markanteil: 60 Prozent.
- Eigenes Lager von Fertigprodukten für 2 Mio. Euro.
- Straßen- und Schienen-DDP-Transportlogistik für Lieferung in alle 14 Regionen des Landes.
- Weiteste Lieferungsentfernung: 2 895 km (Aktau).
- Verkaufsergebnis: 200 km Rohrprodukte unterschiedlicher Durchmesser, sowie ca. 10 000 Formstücke.

Isoplus Central Asia LLP ist der einzige Hersteller von vorgedämmten Rohren und Anbieter von Dienstleistungen für die Isolierung von Rohrverbindungen (Füllen von Kupplungen mit Polyurethan-Schaum), und zwar durch den Einsatz von eigenem mobilen Gerät auf der Basis eines VW Kraftfahrzeugs. Für die qualitativ hochwertige Isolierung von Rohrverbindungen steht unser speziell ausgebildeter Installateur bereit, um sich zur Baustelle zu begeben und den Hohlraum der Kupplung mit einer mobilen Installation für die Isolierung von Kupplungen zu füllen.

(Aus dem Englischen übersetzt von S. Mueller)

Isoplus Central Asia LLP
4 Republic Avenue
590-591 Karaganda, Kazakhstan
📞 +7 (7212) 78 24 84,
   +7 (7212) 78 88 41,
   +7 (701) 801-85-17
✉ kim.a@tooksm.kz
🌐 tooksm.kz

Erst wenn wir die lokale Mentalität verstanden haben und genug Geduld mitbringen, können wir erfolgreich sein.

Interview mit Herrn Leonard Stein, General Manager, Isoplus Central Asia LLP

CCP: *Wir begrüßen Sie, verehrter Herr Stein, zu diesem Interview und danken Ihnen im Voraus dafür, etwas von den Erfahrungen der Firma Isoplus in Kasachstan mit den Lesern dieses Buches zu teilen. Ihre Firma ist seit 2014 mit einem Werk zur Produktion von isolierten Röhrensystemen erfolgreich in Kasachstan tätig. Das manifestiert sich gewiss im Wachstum der Belegschaft. Sie starteten mit wenigen Mitarbeitern, und wie viele Mitarbeiter sind heute für Isoplus in Karaganda tätig?*

LS: Seit dem Start der Produktion in Kasachstan in 2014 hat sich die Anzahl der Belegschaft mehr als verdreifacht. Heute sind bei Isoplus 150 Mitarbeiter tätig. Tendenz steigend.

CCP: *In Kasachstan werden mehrere Sprachen gesprochen, wie ist der Sprachgebrauch in Ihrer Firma?*

LS: Wir haben mehrsprachige Mitarbeiter. Eine Konzernsprache haben wir jedoch nicht. Es hat sich so ergeben, dass etwa 20 Prozent der Belegschaft sehr gut deutsch spricht und ohne Probleme mit deutschen Kollegen kommunizieren kann. Englisch ist auch sehr wichtig, da wir weltweit einkaufen und bereits exportieren wollen.

CCP: *Haben Sie auch deutsche Mitarbeiter?*

LS: Da wir bereits ein gewisses Niveau in der Produktion erreicht haben, können wir auf die ständige Präsenz unserer deutschen Kollegen verzichten. Wie schon gesagt, etwa 20 Prozent unserer Mitarbeiter sind deutschsprachig.

CCP: *Der deutsche direkte Kommunikationsstil verursacht in asiatischer Umgebung mit generell indirektem Kommunikationsstil oft Reibung. Wird das durch den Gebrauch des Englischen ausgeglichen?*

LS: In Kasachstan, wie in den anderen zentralasiatischen Ländern, wird unsere Direktheit inzwischen akzeptiert, da die Partner auch nur sehr wenig Zeit zum Diskutieren haben.

CCP: *Wie schon angedeutet, Kasachstan ist ein Land großer ethnischer und auch religiöser Vielfalt. Wie gehen Sie bei der Personalbeschaffung damit um?*

LS: Beide angedeutete Faktoren spielen dabei absolut keine Rolle. Wir engagieren Mitarbeiter, die das erforderliche fachliche Wissen nachweisen können und genug Motivation bringen

CCP: *Wenn auch vor allem die Qualifikation eines Kandidaten für die Einstellung in Ihrem Werk von Bedeutung ist, so kommen doch mit der kulturellen Vielfalt unterschiedliche Vorstellungen von Unternehmensleitung und Umgang mit Mitarbeitern in Ihrem Werk zusammen. Entstehen dadurch nicht Konflikte?*

LS: Nein, ich wiederhole, fachliches Wissen ist prioritär.

CCP: *Welcher Führungsstil wird in Ihrem Werk in Karaganda praktiziert: ein deutscher, ein Isoplus hauseigener oder ein kasachischer?*

LS: Es ist ein Mix von deutschem und kasachischem Stil.

CCP: *Mit diesem Stil haben Sie also Erfolg. Bitte beschreiben Sie ihn in seinen Grundzügen.*

Isoplus Produkionsanlage in Karaganda, Kasachstan

LS: Akzeptanz, eine bestimmte Freiheit im Treffen von Entscheidungen. Fast unsichtbare Kontrolle

CCP: *Wie ist das Führungsteam zusammengesetzt, kasachisch, kasachisch-deutsch oder international?*

LS: Nur kasachisch

CCP: *War das so von Anfang an oder ist der heutige Stand das Ergebnis von jahrelangen Erfahrungen seit der Eröffnung des Werkes in 2014? Daraus könnten unsere Leser viel lernen.*

LS: Das ist das Ergebnis von jahrelangen Erfahrungen.

CCP: *Nun zwei Fragen zur Arbeitsorganisation: Das Klima in Kasachstan nennen Geographen kontinental, es ist also im Sommer sehr warm bis heiß und im Winter sehr kalt. Hat das einen Einfluss auf die Organisation der Arbeitszeit? Auf die Organisation der Arbeitsprozesse generell?*

LS: Das Klima hat einen enormen Einfluss auf die Struktur und Organisation, angefangen bei unseren Kunden, denn unser Business ist klimabezogen und daher saisonabhängig. Im Winter müssen wir jederzeit damit rechnen, dass wir aufgrund von Kälte oder Schnee keine Ware bekommen oder ausliefern können. Im letzten Winter wurden zum Beispiel insgesamt 36 mal die Straßen gesperrt.

CCP: *Das ist natürlich ganz erheblich. Kommen wir nun zu Ihrer Produktion und dem Arbeitsmarkt in Kasachstan. Finden Sie vor Ort leicht die Fachkräfte, die Sie brauchen?*

LS: Es gibt Positionen, wo wir monatelang brauchen, um eine Fachkraft zu finden. Es ist wirklich sehr schwierig, besonders für ein produzierendes Unternehmen, jemanden zu finden, der unseren Anforderungen entspricht.

CCP: *Die Herstellung Ihrer isolierten Röhrensysteme erfordert sicherlich von den lokalen Führungskräften ebenso wie von den lokalen Mitarbeitern spezielles Wissen, das nur im deutschen Mutterhaus vorhanden ist. Wie kommt es in Ihr Werk in Karaganda?*

LS: Fast alle unsere Mitarbeiter wurden in Deutschland und auch von den Kollegen aus Deutschland vor Ort in Karaganda ausgebildet. Das ist sehr wichtig und an dieser Stelle möchten wir nicht sparen.

CCP: *Führen Sie turnusmäßige Weiterbildungskurse durch und bilden Sie auch Nachwuchskräfte aus?*

LS: Selbstverständlich. Zum jetzigen Zeitpunkt haben wir mehr als zehn Mitarbeiter mit einem zweiten Hochschulabschluss und sogar zwei mit Doktortitel. Weiterbildungskurse finden ständig statt.

CCP: In Kasachstan sind viele ausländische Firmen tätig. Wie motivieren Sie lokale Mitarbeiter, zu Isoplus zu kommen und dann auch zu bleiben?

LS Wir bieten ein sehr gutes Arbeitsklima sowie sehr gute Chancen für Fortbildung und Weiterentwicklung. Außerdem bezahlen wir überdurchschnittlich gut.

CCP: Welche Empfehlungen möchten Sie aufgrund Ihrer langjährigen Erfahrungen und Ihres Erfolgs in Kasachstan künftigen deutschen Mittelständlern auf den Weg geben, um ebenso erfolgreich zu werden bei ihrem Start demnächst in Kasachstan?

LS: Erst wenn wir die lokale Mentalität verstanden haben und genug Geduld mitbringen, können wir erfolgreich sein.

CCP: Vielen Dank, Herr Stein, für dieses Gespräch. Sicherlich vermittelt es weiteren deutschen mittelständischen Firmen als Investoren interessante Einblicke in die Unternehmenstätigkeit in Kasachstan.

Isoplus Central Asia LLP
4 Republic Avenue
590-591 Karaganda, Kazakhstan
📞 +7 (7212) 78 24 84,
   +7 (7212) 78 88 41,
   +7 (701) 801-85-17
✉ kim.a@tooksm.kz
🌐 tooksm.kz

Teil 4

Modernes Kasachstan im Bild

Part 4

Modern Kazakhstan in Pictures

Modernes Kasachstan

Der Bajterek-Turm, Symbol der Unabhängigkeit Kasachstans. / Bajterek Tower, symbol of Kazakhstan's independence. *https://de.wikipedia.org/wiki/Bajterek-Turm, https://en.wikipedia.org/wiki/Baiterek_Tower*

Modern Kazakhstan

Blick vom Bajterek-Turm auf die Hauptstadt Astana / View of the capital Astana from Bayterek Tower *https://de.wikipedia.org/wiki/Astana*

Modernes Kasachstan

Astana: Palast des Präsidenten / Palace of the President

Gebäude des kasachischen Parlaments. / Building of The Kazakh Parliament.

Modern Kazakhstan

Astana: Die *Kazakh Eli* Säule auf dem *Platz der Unabhängigkeit* mit dem mythischen Vogel Samruk an der Spitze, der Frieden, Wohlstand, Kraft und Entwicklung symbolisiert. / The *Kazakh Eli* on Independence Square, with the mythical bird Samruk at the top symbolizing freedom, prosperity, strength and development.

Astana: *Nationalmuseum* auf dem Platz der Unabhängigkeit, das größte Museum Zentralasiens. / *National Museum* on Independence Square, the largest museum in Central Asia.

Modernes Kasachstan

Astana: Das neue *Astana Internationale Finanzzentrum* auf dem Gelände der Expo 2017 / The new *Astana International Finance Center (AIFC)* at the Expo 2017 site.
https://aifc.kz/, https://owc.de/2018/06/12/astana-international-financial-centre-sucht-naehe-deutscher-fintech-unternehmen/, https://en.wikipedia.org/wiki/Astana_International_Financial_Centre

Der *Transport Tower* in der City der Hauptstadt ist der Sitz von zwei Ministerien, auch der staatlichen Verwaltung für internationale Investitionen. / The *Transport Tower* in the capital is the seat of two ministries and of the state administration of international investments.
https://en.wikipedia.org/wiki/List_of_tallest_buildings_in_Astana

Modernes Kasachstan

Astana city center: *Railways Buildings* (175 m), Unternehmenssitz der staatlichen kasachischen Eisenbahn, die höchsten Gebäude Kasachtans / Seat of the *Kazakh State Railway Society*, Kazakhstan's tallest buildings. *https://de.wikipedia.org/wiki/Railways_Building*

Modern Kazakhstan

Astana Opernhaus / The Astana Opera http://astanaopera.kz/en/

Kasachstan Zentrale Konzerthalle / The Kazakhstan Central Concert Hall https://en.wikipedia.org/wiki/Kazakhstan_Central_Concert_Hall;https://www.e-architect.co.uk/kazakhstan/astana-state-auditorium

Modernes Kasachstan

Unabhängigkeitspalast, das nationale Kultur- und Kongress-Zentrum für staatliche Events. / *Independence Palace*, the national cultural and convention center for government events. https://en.wikipedia.org/wiki/Independence_Square,_Astana

Der *Shabyt Kreativitätspalast* auf dem Platz der Unabhängigkeit / The *Shabyt Art Palace* on Independence Square. https://en.wikipedia.org/wiki/Independence_Square,_Astana

Modern Kazakhstan

Atyrau Kopiri – Astanas neuste Fußgängerbrücke, eröffnet im Juli 2018. / *Atyrau Kopiri:* Astana's newest pedestrian bridge, inaugurated in July 2018. https://www.youtube.com/watch?v=EEl2qmXQ4uE

Modernes Kasachstan

Amphitheater am Ufer des Ishim Flusses / Amphitheatre on the banks of the Ishim River.

Nazarbajev Zentrum, Bibliothek des ersten Präsidenten der Republik Kasachstan / Nazarbayev Center, library of the Republic Kasazakhstan's first president. *https://en.wikipedia.org/wiki/Nazarbayev_Center*

Modern Kazakhstan

Wohnhäuser und Bürogebäude am *Nurzhol Boulevard* in Astana. / Residential and office buildings on Astana's *Nurzhol Boulevard.* https://en.wikipedia.org/wiki/Nurzhol_Boulevard

Modernes Kasachstan

Astana: Shopping Center *Keruen City* mit einer Restaurant- und Kino-Etage und *Khan Schatyr* Einkaufs- und Unterhaltungszentrum mit einem Strandbad unter dem zeltartigen transparenten Dach. / The *Keruen City* shopping mall includes a food court and movie theatre while the Khan Schatyr Entertainment Center has a beach under its translucent tent-like roof. *https://www.edgekz.com/what-to-do/astana/shopping*

Modern Kazakhstan

Modernste Monitor überwachte Produktionsanlagen von Hühnerfleisch der Managing Company Schanyrak in Akmola, in der Nähe von Astana. / Modern computer-controlled processing plant for chicken meat products at the Managing Company Schanyrak in Akmola, near Astana.

Modernes Kasachstan

Aktivitäten der Amazone-Werke in Kasachstan: Pflanzen Check durch Dr. Meinel, Schulung kasachischer Landwirte und Feldtag als Teil des Schulungsprogramms. / Amazone activities in Kazakhstan: Dr. Meinel inspects the plants. The continuing education of Kazakh farmers includes a field day as part of the qualification program.

Modern Kazakhstan

Die Steinkohlenförderung prägt auch heute noch das Landschaftsbild sowie das Wirtschaftsprofil der Region um Karaganda. / Coal mining even today characterizes the landscape as well as the economic profile of the Qaraghandy Region.

Karaganda: Das *Haus der Bergleute* ist ein bedeutendes Kulturzentrum der Stadt / The *Miners Cultural Palace* is an important cultural center in the city. https://de.wikipedia.org/wiki/Qaraghandy

Modernes Kasachstan

Karaganda, Stadtzentrum. / Qaraghandy, city centre.

Die große moderne Eissporthalle ermöglicht Wintersport auch im Sommer. / The large modern ice-skating rink makes winter sports even possible in the summer.

Die größte Stadt Kasachstans, *Almaty*, liegt am Fuße des Alatau-Gebirges mit 3-400 m hohen ganzjährig schneebedeckten Gipfeln. / Kazakhstan's largest city, *Almaty,* is located at the foot of the year-round, snow-capped Alatau Mountains, approx. 9 800 to 13 000 feet high. *https://en.wikipedia.org/wiki/Almaty*

Das Eissportzentrum *Medeu* in 2000 m Höhe gehört zu den größten der Welt. – Mit ihren zahlreichen Parks mit Wasserspielen gehört Almaty zu den grünsten Städten der Welt. / The *Medeu* outdoor ice-skating and bandy rink at an altitude of 6 500 feet is one of the largest in the world. – With its numerous parks with fountains, Almaty is one of the greenest cities in the world.

Modernes Kasachstan

Die weißen spitzen Türme des brandneuen gläsernen *Business Centre Nurly Tau* in Almaty konkurrieren mit schneebedeckten Gebirgsgipfeln gegenüber am Horizont. / The white pointed towers of the brand-new Business Center *Nurly Tau* with glass fronts in Almaty compete with the snow-capped mountain peaks on the horizon opposite. https://www.bigstockphoto.com/de/image-186351394/stock-photo-almaty-business-center-nurly-tau

Almaty ist das größte Wirtschafts- und Kulturzentrum Kasachstans. Hier im Bild ein moderner Restaurant – und Convention-Komplex an der Dostyk Avenue. / Almaty is Kazakhtan's most important economic and cultural center. In the picture a modern restaurant and convention complex on Dostyk Avenue.

Modern Kazakhstan

MEGA International in Almaty ist das größte Shopping und Entertainment Center Zentralasiens. / *MEGA International* in Almaty is the largest shopping and entertainment mall in Central Asia. https://de.wikipedia.org/wiki/Mega_Center_Alma-Ata

Viele Sprachen der Welt im Straßenbild von Almaty zeugen davon, dass die frühere Hauptstadt auch die kosmopolitischste des Landes ist. / The many languages of the world in Alamaty's streets bear witness to the former capital's reputation as the country's most cosmopolitan city.

Modernes Kasachstan

Die DKU ist die einzige internationale Universität in Zentralasien, die nach deutschen Standards unterrichtet. Zu unseren Lehrkräften gehören deutsche und kasachische Professoren und Praktiker.

Wenn Sie vorhaben, einen Studienaufenthalt zu absolvieren, eine Hochschulausbildung, ein Praktikum oder einen Forschungsaufenthalt in Kasachstan zu machen, stehen Ihnen die Türen der DKU offen! Die Internationale Abteilung unserer Universität informiert Sie umfassend über die Studienbedingungen an der DKU, die Zulassungsvoraussetzungen (Visum, Zulassung, Versicherung) und über Sprachkurse. Bei Bedarf helfen wir bei Wohnungssuche in Almaty.

dku.kz/de

Modern Kazakhstan

Die beiden Memorials in Schymkent, der Millionenstadt im Süden Kasachstans, verbinden Geschichte und Gegenwart: während die drei Stelen mit Landesprofil der modernen unabhängigen Republik gewidmet sind, dokumentiert das symbolhafte Jurten-Denkmal die Gründung der Stadt an der Seidenstraße durch Kasachen im 12. Jahrhundert. / The two monuments in the southern main city of Shymkent connect the past and present while the monument with the columns and map of Kazakhstan is dedicated to the modern independent republic. The symbolic yurt monument documents the founding of the city on the Silk Road in the 12th century by the Kazakhs. *https://de.wikipedia.org/wiki/Schymkent*

Schymkent: Die weltgrößte Tulpe steht in der Fontäne im Stadtzentrum. Sie hat historischen Hintergrund. / Shymkent: The world's largest tulip is in the fountain in the city centre. It has a historical background. *http://www.tulipstore.eu/de/tulpen/geschichte-der-tulpe/*

Modernes Kasachstan

Schymkent ist ein bedeutender Eisenbahnknotenpunkt an der Turkestan-Sibirien-Linie, die nördlich von Taschkent beginnt und in Barnaul in Russland endet. / Shymkent is a major railroad junction on the Turkestan–Siberian Railway that starts north of Tashkent and ends in Barnaul, Russia. https://en.wikipedia.org/wiki/Shymkent

Der *Royal Club* ist nach einem älteren Aquapark das modernste Sport und Spa Center der Stadt. / The *Royal Club* is the latest and most modern sports and spa center of the city after the Shymkent Aquapark. http://royalfitness.kz

Das *Schymkent Plaza* ist das beste und bei den Einwohnern beliebteste Shopping und Entertainment Center des modernen Schymkent. Kasachische Symbole charakterisieren die Innenarchitektur. / The *Shymkent Plaza* is the best and most popular shopping and entertainment center in the modern Shymkent. Kazakh symbols are featured in the interior design. http://www.tsd.kz/en/projects/shymkent-plaza

Mehrere moderne Neubaugebiete entsprechen dem ständigen Bevölkerungswachstum dieser südlichen Metropole, nahe der Grenze zu Usbeskistan / Several new modern urban areas correspond to Shymkent's permanent population growth, the southern metropolitain city located near the Uzbek border. https://www.novastan.org/de/kasachstan/das-pralle-leben-in-schymkent

Part 1

Kazakhstan Today

Exceptionally great changes planned for the economic structure in Kazakhstan

Interview with Prof. Dr. Wilhelm Bender, former Chairman, Executive Board, Fraport AG, Independent Director, Member of the Board of Directors of Sovereign Wealth Fund Samruk-Kazyna Joint Stock Company, Kazakhstan

CCP: Professor Bender, you have many responsibilities, so to begin with, thank you very much for your willingness to do this interview for MODERN KAZAKHSTAN. I understand you know Kazakhstan quite well. Could you tell me some of the characteristics of developed Kazakhstan that spontaneously come to mind based on your travels?

PWB: I had absolutely no idea of Kazakhstan. First of all, I learned how large this country is. Its size naturally creates relative challenges in supplying the population, the infrastructure, mobility, etc. – challenges that the leadership and the national companies need to master.

In this respect, it is especially impressive what the state intends to achieve in the way of growth and modernization.

CCP: Yes, it is indeed very impressive and the state government has major plans for its further development. This is why they are calling upon the know-how of foreign experts such as you. Why actually? Certainly there are experts with a lot of international experience available domestically.

PWB: The government and the state fund are looking for external expert knowledge for good reasons. They want to make use of our knowledge in, for example, going public and restructuring companies under high time pressure. In doing so, they will definitely shape the country.

CCP: That is understandable. Next, could you tell us something about your professional background, Professor.

PWB: First, I was the CEO at Fraport in Frankfurt for 17 years including going public in 2001. Before that, I was the CEO at Schenker shipping services. Then, in addition I have a broad range of AR experience at ThyssenKrupp Services, Adtranz, Bombardier, Techem, Signal Iduna, LH Cargo, MTU, among others. Finally, I also have volunteer experience in economic development.

CCP: You have a very convincing profile, Professor. Currently, the Kazakh government asked for your support in modernizing the country. Which reforms have been planned there?

PWB: Great, really major reforms in the economic structure have been mapped out. So, there is, for example, privatization through sales, partial sales and IPOs. In addition, internationally tried and true standards in company management, in the organization of firms and their organs will be decided on and implemented. That means governance and compliance regulations.

CCP: These are encouraging objectives. Yet, they certainly will not be easy to put into reality. What above everything else has to be achieved?

PWB: The state quota in the companies needs to be reduced drastically. The state government wants to withdraw totally or partially from key enterprises. This is not something that can be done by just pressing a button. We know that from the structural changes we went through. The non-executive and independent directors – so me, for example – are closely involved in the corporate activity in line with their board membership.

CCP: Privatization is an important process that is also carefully observed from abroad.

PWB: That is right. It is perhaps even the most significant process in modernization. For this purpose, you will need to wrestle for acceptance internally – in society, in the companies. Change in general, mainly privatization, must be viewed as an opportunity and be supported. It should not be seen as a threat to one's own status. This is very difficult in the communication process, yet it is necessary. Once it is successful, trust from the outside grows.

CCP: Kazakhstan needs a new image, isn't that true?

PWB: Yes, and it can only be achieved through internal reforms. As a result, acceptance by foreign investors will rise and then the international capital market, the investors as well as politics will be convinced. Opening the International Finance Center to this end is certainly an important step in the right direction.

CCP: Could you describe how you go about influencing economic change?

PWB: In early March, Prime Minister Bakytzhan Sagintayev invited me to become a member of the board at Samruk-Kazyna, a giant state fund. This fund owns the postal service and the railroad; the oil and gas corporation KazMunay Gaz; the uranium company; Air Astana; the airports; and many other large companies – practically everything that is critical for the nation, its infrastructure and the interaction of the economy. The stock market value for Samruk-Kazyna amounts to more than USD 100 billion. In comparison, the value for the Deutsche Bank is EUR 22 billion, Daimler-Benz EUR 78 billion and for Lufthansa EUR 12 billion.

CCP: That really is a tremendous value. And how does this fund operate?

PWB: In Kazakhstan, the one-tier system is in effect. That means the uniform board of directors consists of executive and non-executive members. So there is no separate board of directors and a supervisory board as we have in Germany. The Anglo-Saxon system is valid there. For the non-executive and independent directors, so, for example, I have a greater influence and am more involved in corporate activities.

CCP: How many people are on the board?

PWB: The Samruk-Kazyna board consists of the prime minister as chair, the finance minister, the economics minister, the CEO of the fund and three independent directors including myself. So, it is not under the full power of the government. The most important board committee, the audit committee, is comprised only of the independent directors and all three are foreigners.

CCP: So, will you be playing a crucial role in the privatization process?

PWB: Yes, and it not only means privatizing the infrastructure companies, which is an absolutely essential goal of the president and the government. This measure opens up considerable opportunities for western investors: on the one hand, for participating in companies; on the other hand, there are also opportunities for suppliers. Economic growth will in addition reinforce Kazakh consumer capabilities. The country requires a stable domestic demand for sustainable success.

CCP: President Nasarbajev pursues the goal of leading Kazakhstan to become one of the 30 strongest developed nations in the world by 2050. What else needs to be done to achieve this target once privatization has been completed?

PWB: Further necessary changes are setting up future-oriented, strong-growth industries, reducing the dependency of raw material industries and reinforcing the services sector. The curricula as well as the general mindset will have to change as well.

CCP: The vehicles of the future are the country's young people. What is your opinion of Kazakhstan's new generation?

PWB: Kazakhstan is a nation undergoing development. This is true for the leadership, economic elite as well as the people that I have met. The new generation is highly motivated and excellently educated, often in foreign countries. They know that their advancement depends on their own performance.

I am willing to make my contribution for change in Kazakhstan, yet also to awaken the interest of German investors in this country.

CCP: Thank you, Professor, for your convincing statement. You have a large task ahead that is also an opportunity in forming modern Kazakhstan with your know-how. We wish you every success.

Prof. Dr. Wilhelm Bender
✉ w.bender@frankfurt-airportoffice.de

German companies in high demand as investors in Kazakhstan

By Mr. Peter Tils, Co-Chairman of the German-Kazakh Business Council

The Republic of Kazakhstan started to co-operate closely with multinational partners very early to embark on an ambitious economic program. At the beginning of its transformation process in the early nineties, this former Soviet republic already invited international investors to develop and expand its oil and gas resources with non-traditional know-how, insofar creating strong competition for the local oil industry and stepping up efficiency. Oil and gas companies from China, France, Italy, Russia, the UK, US and other countries have been present here for years. President Nazarbayev founded the *Foreign Investors Council (FIC)* that facilitated a permanent dialogue with foreign investors and led to a broad range of investor-friendly regulatory and political decisions. This was the basis for the significant, partially double-digit growth rates that Kazakhstan's economy demonstrated from the middle of the nineties to the financial crisis in 2007/8 and the following years until the oil crisis in 2013-15. In addition, Kazakhstan had provided well against the risk of economic downturns by creating an oil reserve fund that was used in times of need. Today the nation has a stock of approx. USD 300 bn through direct foreign investments, has returned to growth rates of approx. 4 percent and is looking forward optimistically.

Having focused on its vast natural resources in the past, Kazakhstan is currently concentrating on taking the financial sector to new levels. Since hosting the Expo 2017, the country has been developing its *Astana International Financial Center (AIFC)* based on its new and impressive expo infrastructure. Again, this country is internationalizing its economy.

Current positive economic advances by important neighbors, its integration into regional co-operation organizations, such as the *Eurasian*

Economic Union or the *Central Asian Co-operation*, will allow Astana to further blend into the regional and global financial system. The AIFC will be governed by a special legal framework based on English law. A regulatory system with a focus on transparency and investor protection was established. A special tax framework is designed to support the financial center's positive development. Collaboration with the *Shanghai Stock Exchange* and the *NASDAQ American Stock Exchange* has been designed to attract foreign experience and know-how. The AIFC will focus on capital markets, asset management, commercial technologies, Islamic economics and private banking. It is the only international financial center of its kind in the *CIS (Commonwealth of Independent States)*. The official launch was celebrated at an impressive event on July 5, 2018, together with a newly created conference, the *Astana Finance Days*. The event allowed for an intensive dialogue with national and international partners on the expectations for the new AIFC, global trends in finance and regional developments. The conference and the official opening left an impression of how seriously Kazakhstan has implemented this new tool for the sound and stable economic development of this country and its people.

An important issue still to be resolved is which assets will be traded in Astana and how to generate the necessary liquidity for various capital market instruments. The key to its success will be the third privatization round announced by the government. The first corporations to be listed on the newly created *Astana Stock Exchange* include *Kazatomprom, Air Astana* and *Kaz-Telekom*. Important Kazakh companies, such as *Kazmunaigaz*, are planned to follow soon. In addition, there is a discussion on registering certain bonds in the context of the AIFC. This is a prerequisite in providing the liquidity needed for an attractive financial center where international asset managers, state reserve funds and private individuals are active. There were rumors at the opening that even Chinese companies might be listed, which would certainly fuel liquidity further. If this all comes together through the willingness of future regional partners close to Astana, then the chances for success for the new AIFC are good.

Germany and its vibrant economy have always been a focus of interest to the Kazakh government. German immigrants played a positive role in the development of Soviet Kazakhstan, and especially, President Nazarbayev appreciates their contributions. After Germany reunified, more than 700 000 Germans left Kazakhstan. Their contributions were missed in rebuilding the nation after independence from the Soviet Union. Today, Kazakhstan is keen on attracting German companies to invest in the country.

While Germany has not been strong in the oil and gas sector for historical reasons, Kazakhstan anticipates German companies will help in further diversifying their economy. The developments in 2013 when commodity prices deteriorated especially in the oil industry led to substantial efforts for intensified diversification. German industry know-how was designed to help in this case. In 2010, the *German-Kazakh Business Council* had been founded based on a memorandum of understanding signed during Chancellor Merkel's visit to Astana. The founding members were business associations, such as the *Committee on Eastern European Economic Relations* and the *Eastern Europe Business Association of Germany* (both of whom meanwhile merged into one organization) and the *National Chamber of Entrepreneurs of the Republic of Kazakhstan "Atameken"*. In 2012, the Business Council was then complemented by the partnership agreement in the areas of natural resources and new technologies. Its purpose is to secure access to the country's rich resources in raw materials and rare earth metals for German companies while providing technologies from Germany.

The *German-Kazak Business Council* has met ten times so far. Its goals to support German investments in Kazakhstan and to ensure smooth-running capital projects by the Kazakh side were fully delivered. The Council has discussed and backed implementing numerous investment projects, serves as the platform to address business hurdles and a place to share experiences made in Kazakhstan and Germany. The Council meetings are attended by business representatives from both countries. The discussions take place on concrete matters, often with successful outcomes.

Since 2005, German business in Kazakhstan has amounted to more than USD 3.5 bn and many new projects are in the planning. A positive signal is that many companies reinvest their profits into the country. In this context, we all anticipate that the Euler Hermes coverage that Germany provides for exports will be re-established during the second half of 2018. Their coverage had been ceased in 2008 following the turbulences in the Kazakh banking sector: negotiations to re-establish it last until today. For many companies, this state commitment is crucial in implementing significant investment projects supported by sizable machinery and technological exportation.

Kazakhstan today is placed comparably high in different global indices, for example in competitiveness, central government policy making and tax climate. It currently ranks 29 in human development out of 130 economies. Early on, the government promoted a high level of education including publicly financed scholarships abroad. More than 10 000 students profited from this policy. Most of the younger leaders in politics and the economy are foreign-educated and have good language skills. In one of the key challenges going forward, Kazakhstan has also been actively addressing the digitalization of the economy, developing appropriate initiatives, international co-operation and projects.

In Central Asia, Kazakhstan has been a stabilizing factor in the region for many years. The stable political and economic environment depends on sound and effective succession planning for the governmental leadership of the country. Initial important steps were taken to strengthen the parliament and government for a possible smooth transition in 2020 and the following years. In addition, the *Belt and Road Initiative*, commonly known as the *Silk Road Initiative*, was designed to provide huge infrastructure backing. The AIFC forms one pillar for its financing. With a constantly high global capital flow of approx. USD 27 bn per year, continued international co-operation and continued investments in human capital, the AIFC establishment and the outlook for the Belt and Road Initiative in Kazakhstan's future could be very promising.

Peter Tils
peter-a.tils@db.com

Part 2

Modern Kazakhstan: Attractive Destination for Foreign Investment

The EAEU and the New Silk Road offer excellent long-term market opportunities and make Kazakhstan an ideal site for German companies

Interview with Dr. Robert Breitner, Representative of German Economic Affairs for Central Asia with headquarters in Almaty

CCP: The subject of our interview is modern Kazakhstan. Dr. Breitner, I understand you live in this country and that you have seen the innovations taken place. Could you tell us what in your opinion are the main characteristics of modern-day Kazakhstan?

RB: The first main characteristic is ambition: In 2013, President Nasarbajew announced the *Kazakhstan 2050* strategy. It states the long-term goals for the nation's modernization. The chief target of this course of action is the state's advancement to belong to the group of 30 most developed countries. The cornerstones of Kazakh economic and financial policies are a low debt burden, a realignment of the energy supply, intensified modernization efforts and diversification of the economy. Its purpose is to expand the mining and further processing of raw materials as well as to decrease dependency on crude oil. Particular emphasis is on the development of the manufacturing industry, agriculture and transportation; restructuring the energy sectors; and supporting medium-sized businesses.

Kazakhstan's strong involvement in creating a good economic policy framework was recognized in *Doing Business* by the World Bank, whereby Kazakhstan ranked 35 and is as such in the top group of the CIS (Commonwealth of Independent States).

The second main characteristic is international focus: Kazakhstan's most important, direct trading partners are China and Russia. It is a founding member of the *Eurasian Economic Union (EAEU)*, a member of the *Shanghai Cooperation Organization (SCO)* and participates actively in the Chinese initiative *Silk Road Economic Belt*.

CCP: Due to its location between China and Russia in Central Asia, Kazakhstan is a lucrative site for foreign stakeholders. How does Germany currently rank overall as an investor in Kazakhstan in relationship to the total number of investors from other countries?

RB: Close to 50 percent of all overseas direct investments in late 2017 originated in The Netherlands. One reason for this is that many foreign companies process their financial interests in Kazakhstan through Dutch holdings. With immediate investments in the amount of USD 558 million, Germany ranked 17. According to the Bundesbank, 40 companies had directly financed EUR 225 million in Kazakhstan by the end of 2016.

CCP: Which German companies have been in the country with their production systems the longest and certainly on good grounds?

RB: Among the German companies who have been producing here the longest are the following member firms in The German Industrial Association in Kazakhstan: KNAUF, Henkel, BASF, Böhmer Armatura, Isoplus, ODDESSE (OZA) and more recently, WILO.

CCP: The biggest names are the first German investors everywhere in the world, yet medium-sized firms form the backbone of the economy in Germany and are also valued worldwide. To which extent are these medium-sized companies present in Kazakhstan?

RB: Five of the seven just named are medium-sized manufacturing companies who selected Kazakhstan to produce for Central Asia, Mongolia and partially for the South Caucasus. Furthermore, you will find that of the 100 firms listed in the German Industrial Association in Kazakhstan, there are approx. 70 percent German medium-sized firms who mainly maintain representative offices there.

CCP: What makes Kazakhstan lucrative today as an investment target and site for German medium-sized companies?

RB: Kazakhstan has the strongest performing economy in Central Asia, competitive personnel costs while it has high needs for modernization. Furthermore, the nation is located on the *New Silk Road* between China and Russia and is a member of the EAEU, which also offers medium-sized companies new, untapped market opportunities up to now.

CCP: What do people in Kazakhstan appreciate about German medium-sized companies?

RB: Above all, they appreciate the highly specialized products and services. They furthermore value German long-term commitment to the economy and social involvement for their employees and the region in which they operate.

CCP: *What are some of the projects implemented by German medium-sized companies that significantly contributed to the nation's modern image during the past three to five years?*

RB: There is, for example, the highway construction from Astana to Borovoe in Kazakhstan by GP Papenburg Baugesellschaft mbH or a 4-km stretch of underground shaft out of a total of 12 km for chrome ore mining in the country's northwest by TOO SCHACHTBAU Kazakhstan.

CCP: *In which sectors of Kazakhstan's economy are innovative German medium-sized business currently very much in demand?*

RB: Based on its large geographic area and need for modernization, the country is above all interested in specialty suppliers of railway, port, aeronautics and roadway construction technologies; however, technology suppliers for the development and expansion of crude oil, natural gas, pipelines, power plants as well as logistics companies are in high demand. In addition, Kazakhstan wants to become gradually more independent of agricultural and food imports by placing a greater emphasis on locally processed food products. This is why Kazakhstan is also interesting for the food companies along with the processing machinery. An added advantage for this sector is that China as a further possible export market is located in the regional vicinity.

CCP: *Culturally, Kasakhstan is so different in comparison to Germany. What should German managers acting as representatives in Kazakhstan in the near future be aware of to be successful right from the start?*

RB: In order to work successfully in Kazakhstan and Central Asia, it is important to be patient, listen well and maintain social contact to employees and partners. Any type of business in Kazakhstan, as everywhere in the world, begins with a good personal relationship and good command of the languages of partners and employees is an advantage in the country.

CCP: *Business people also have a personal life and interests. This is why your personal experience is interesting. What do you personally like about your life in Almaty and Kazakhstan?*

RB: I came to Kazakhstan only a short while ago and live in Almaty. I very much appreciate the mountains there that offer recreation opportunities all year round, especially hiking and skiing.

CCP: *Dr. Breitner, thank you very much for this interview. It will certainly provide future German investors with interesting insights and assist them in targeting finance opportunities for a modern Kazakhstan.*

Representative of German Economic Affairs for Central Asia

Business Center "Koktem Square"
Bostandykski rayon
Mkr. Koktem 1, dom 15 a
050040 Almaty, Kazakhstan
📞 +7 727 35610 -61 62 63 64 65
✉ info@ahk-za.com
🌐 www.ahka-za.com

**Delegation der Deutschen
Wirtschaft für Zentralasien
Представительство Германской
экономики в Центральной Азии**

Kazakhstan offers excellent opportunities for investors

By Hans-Joachim Bischoff,
Representative Germany,
KAZAKH INVEST

Kazakhstan, the ninth-largest country in the world, is centrally located on the Silk Road. Interest in economic relations with Kazakhstan has been growing steadily, since the republic offers favorable conditions for investors and overland trade routes. For example, a stakeholder may receive official financial assistance of up to 30 percent. In addition, the steps to diversify the economy described in the president's program are based on a long-term and reliable strategy.

As recently as 2016, Kazakhstan faced challenges connected to low commodity prices. The fiscal support and structural reforms implemented by the Kazakh government since then have helped to improve the economic situation. The renewal process for the Kazakh economy has been activated and, as a result, GDP grew 4 percent in 2017.

Business climate improved significantly

In 2017, business between Germany and the region increased noticeably: bilateral trade with Kazakhstan climbed by 23 percent to approx. EUR 5 billion. Kazakhstan is the most important economic partner in Central Asia for German firms. Despite its abundance of raw materials, the country pursues a clear modernization strategy. In technical and innovative renewal, especially German companies are seen as a desired partner.

In Kazakhstan, state-owned KAZAKH INVEST has been responsible for official support measures in industrial and innovation processes, investor recruitment and location marketing since 2017. With a new strategy package, the country is aiming for an increase in industrial exports. In addition, it is driving the modernization of the economy forward based on the Digitalization of Kazakhstan program. Despite strong dependency on commodity prices, growth is expected to lie between 3.1 percent and 4.2 percent according to the socio-economic forecast for 2018-2022.

About Kazakhstan

Name:	Republic of Kazakhstan
Founded:	December 16, 1991
Government:	Unitary presidential constitutional republic
President:	Nursultan Nazarbayev
Official Languages:	Kazakh (state language) and Russian
Capital:	Astana
Area:	1 694 563 square miles (ninth largest country in the world)
Administrative sites:	14 regions and 3 cities of national importance: Astana (population: approx. 1 million) Almaty (population: approx. 1.7 million) Shymkent (population: approx. 1 million)
Population:	Approx. 18 million
Population density:	Approx. 16.8/square mile
Currency:	Tenge (KZT) 1 KZT= 0.002 EUR; 1 EUR = 407.6 KZT
Time Zone:	GMT West/East + 5/+6
International Calling Code:	+7
Internet TLD:	.kz
Country Code/ ISO 3166:	KZ
National Holiday:	December 16

On the basis of moderate growth rates in the global economy, a rebound in demand will develop and the maintenance of low commodity prices. Kazakhstan will continue to be by far Germany's largest business partner in Central Asia.

Sustaining a favorable investment climate and promoting foreign direct investment in the economy are two of the most important tasks. The aim of the State Program for Industrial and Innovative Development of the Republic of Kazakhstan for the period 2015 to 2019 is to promote the competitiveness of the processing industry based on labor productivity and the rise in export volumes of processed goods. Attracting investments, also from abroad, plays a significant role. Foreign direct investment is mainly focused on the chemical and pharmaceutical industries, engineering, construction, transportation and mining of metal ores.

Promoting and processing the country's natural resources are still worthwhile; above all, oil and gas, yet also uranium, copper, zinc, iron ore, etc. According to *Trading Economics* estimates, investments in the amount of USD 5.5 billion were expected for the second quarter of 2018. Already during the first quarter of 2018, USD 5.16 billion had been invested. Demand in agriculture and the food industry is rising. In addition, the energy sector and trading harbor potential for German investors.

Digitalization drives German-Kazakh relations

Kazakhstan goal is to rank among the 30 strongest economies in the world by 2050. This would require an annual growth rate of approx. 5 percent. Although the nation as the largest in Central Asia is blessed with the wealth of raw materials, such a goal cannot be achieved on this basis alone. The Kazakh government is therefore focusing on further growth drivers, including digitalization in keeping with the spirit of the times. The industrial sectors, above all mining and heavy industry, are to become more competitive and profitable thanks to Industry 4.0.

Note the following before investing:

1. Inform yourself first

An initial discussion with KAZAKH INVEST makes sense. *Hans-Joachim Bischoff* is available as the contact person in Germany.

2. Payment processes with Kazakh banks

German companies should pay attention to the processing of payments. The procedure of just opening a bank account can take several weeks

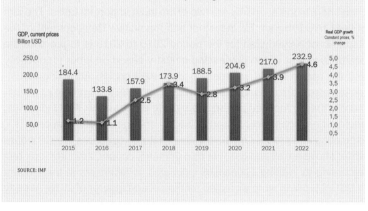

Why invest in Kasakhstan?

BUSINESS-FRIENDLY ENVIRONMENT

SOCIAL/ECONOMIC STABILITY

ATTRACTIVENESS FOR INVESTMENT

SUSTAINABLE HIGH GROWTH

INCOME EQUALITY

FAVORABLE TAX CLIMATE

ACCESS TO THE MAIN REGIONAL MARKETS

EXPERIENCED AND TRAINED WORKFORCE

STATE SUPPORT

and require considerable effort for the notarization of signature cards, transmission of electronic signature devices, etc. Kazakh financial institutions often request copies of contracts or invoices for settlement and to comply with foreign currency regulations. Therefore, be aware that funds cannot be transferred overnight, especially if employees from accounting as authorized representatives need to approve payment. Due to the time difference of four to five hours, plan and closely coordinate such transactions with the subsidiary.

3. Customs Code of the Eurasian Economic Union

On January 1, 2018, the new Customs Code of the *Eurasian Economic Union (CC EAEU)* came into force. It is based on advanced customs practices, including the provisions of the *Kyoto Convention* on the Simplification of Harmonization of Customs Procedures and the Bali *Agreement of the World Trade Organization* on the simplification of trade procedures.

An important advantage of the Customs Code is that relationships along with legal connections have been clearly established. This way, every economic enterprise knows its rights and obligations. Subjectivity was excluded in the decision-making processes of the customs authorities by using information systems and technologies. By barring regulatory conflicts — both directly in customs and in other areas of legislation — there will be less uncertainty leading to financial losses for investors, which can have a major impact on the outcome of a project.

The CC EAEU has minimized the capital risks in terms of taxes and penalties. It is expected that the Custom Code's innovative nature will increase the volume of trade and promote the development of the economy within the *Economic Union*.

Many international companies moving to Kazakhstan

The country is attracting foreign companies through drastically reduced structural costs and relatively mild legal conditions. Today, the Kazakh government is focusing on domestic economic stimulus plans, such as the *Nurly Zhol* and the *Digitalization of Kazakhstan*. In addition, improvements in the investment climate, the competitive environment and the promotion of innovation activities are expected as part of the "100 concrete steps to implement the 5 institutional reforms".

The private sector needs to become one of the main sources of

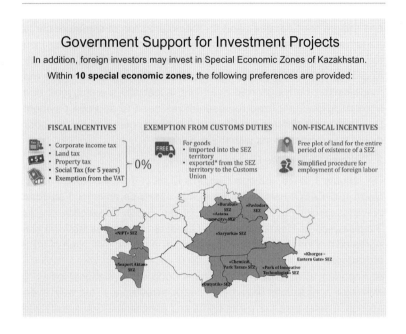

economic growth. To this end, measures will be taken to reduce all types of management costs. State service delivery procedures will be optimized and digitalized as far as possible.

To improve the business environment, tax and customs reforms are planned. In addition, the opening and registration procedures for new companies will be simplified and the rights of minority shareholders strengthened.

Despite dependence on commodity exports, Kazakhstan is generally on the right road to positive economic and political development.

Opening Astana International Financial Center

At the beginning of the year, the *Astana International Financial Center (AIFC)* started operations. The financial center under the patronage of President Nursultan Nazarbayev is part of Kazakhstan's strategy to secure its place among the 30 largest economies in the world. The new financial center is located on the modern premises of the Expo 2017 in the nation's capital Astana.

Representatives of the German economy welcomed the founding of the financial center. Michael Harms, managing director of the German Eastern Business Association, said in an interview, "German companies could invest much more in Kazakhstan and we have to work harder to create joint projects." For Germany, it is important to support stakeholders and to ensure stable business conditions. The center will play a key role in future foreign backing.

Foreign direct investment in Kazakhstan, which amounted to USD 5 381 billion in 2017, has put the post-Soviet republic in 36th place, according to the World Bank's ease of doing business index.

The aim of the *Astana International Financial Center* is to be an institution that conforms to international standards and governs relations between companies according to the principles of common law. In addition, a financial court is to be created, which is responsible for deciding on disputes and investment issues. The center also offers a number of benefits to resident firms.

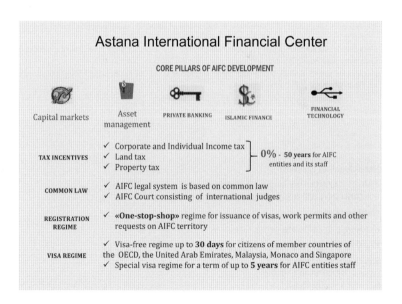

Planned benefits for foreign companies as investors are:
- Exemption from corporate income tax,
- Exemption from income tax for resident employees,
- Reimbursement of VAT for foreign workers,
- Abolition of the work permit requirement for foreign employees.

For 2018, far-reaching privatization projects have commenced. The AIFC is now intended to be the center for attracting investment and a respectable place in the international financial system.

Hans-Joachim Bischoff has represented KAZAKH INVEST in Germany since 01.01.2018. KAZAKH INVEST offers services to support investment projects in Kazakhstan, from idea to implementation on a one-stop-shop basis and is free for investors.

Hans-Joachim Bischoff has held various board positions in his career and is managing director of NEXT STEP Personal in Hannover.

His career began with management positions in financial market and online communications companies with a national and international focus. The communication expert supported this with his profound knowledge in the areas of financial communication and investor relations.

Particularly successful were various investments and international investment projects in Germany and South Africa.

He was successfully responsible for several IPOs and capital increases of listed companies as *Head of Investor Relations*.

Hans-Joachim Bischoff

INVEST KAZAKH Representative Germany
"KAZAKH INVEST" National Company JSC

Germany Office:

Krackeweg 6, 30559 Hannover, Germany

Kazakhstan Office:

2 Kunayev st., 7th floor,
Astana, Kazakhstan 010000
📞 + 49 511 300 89 90
📶 + 49 178 72 58 68 0
✉ bischoff@invest.gov.kz
🌐 www.invest.gov.kz

The legal basis for business with Kazakh partners

By Prof. Dr. Hans-Joachim Schramm and Dimitri Olejnik, Ostinstitut Wismar, Germany

1. The Kazakh Constitution

The Kazakh legal system is based on the Constitution of Kazakhstan dated August 30, 1995 and was adopted by referendum. It contains all the institutions and concepts that may be found in the corresponding documents of western countries:

- Fundamental rights,
- Separation of powers,
- The rule of law,
- Democracy,
- Independent justice and
- The welfare state.

After all, in the World Justice Report 2017-2018 Kazakhstan occupies the second-best place among all the successor states of the Soviet Union in terms of rule of law. From an entrepreneurship point of view, the Constitution stresses the right to free enterprise and the continued existence of state ownership of land and resources. These regulations are in line with the findings of World Bank authors that in Kazakhstan, a large proportion of enterprises, especially in the central sectors of natural resources, energy, transport, water and communications, are still state-owned.

2. The Kazakh business legal framework

In the business legal framework, a strong orientation towards the Russian legal framework exists, yet which has recently been overlaid by Anglo-Saxon influences. The orientation towards the Russian judicial system is based on close relations between the two countries, both in cultural and economic terms. This indirectly leads to numerous links and identical legal concepts in Kazakh and European law, since the authors of the Russian Civil Code had decided in favor of the continental European judicial system. The distinguished symbol of this close connection to the Russian legal framework is the *Kazakh Civil Code* of December 27, 1994 (Part 1) and July 1, 1999 (Part 2): it is related to the Russian Civil Code and even a German attorney will easily recognize similarities. The *Civil Code* contains basic regulations on contract law, property law, (in deviation from the BGB) provisions on intellectual property and conflict of laws (international private law). However, the relevance of special legislation, such as consumer protection, banking contracts and collateral, is growing. Means of secured transactions, such as liens and mortgages, are also regulated in separate pieces of legislation. Titles on land and immovable property are defined in the *Land Code* and recorded in the *Register of Immovable Property*. In this context, it is noteworthy that Kazakhstan received an above-average grade in the World Bank's *Doing Business Report 2018* (DBR 2018) in the area of contract performance and registration of property.

3. US influence in corporation and capital market law

There is a strong US influence reflected in the corporation and capital market law. The central legal document in this respect is the *Law on Corporations* of May 13, 2003, which is based on the model of a US corporation. Remarkably, the minimum capital required of a Kazakh corporation is set at more than USD 340 million. In the end, this piece of legislation has brought Kazakhstan the best rating worldwide in the DBR 2018 category "Protection of minority shareholders".

For medium-sized investors, the German limited liability company (GmbH) is mirrored in the cooperative (tovarishtshestvo) of limited liability that is stipulated in the *Law on TOO* of April 22, 1998. This legal form is only partly equivalent to a GmbH in Germany, since shareholders can be held accountable by the creditors in the event of a negative balance (Art. 25 (3) Law on TOO). There is a register, however, that serves a different function compared to the commercial register in Germany.

The most obvious reference to Anglo-Saxon models is the *Creation of the Astana International Financial Center*, by a constitutional law dated December 7, 2015. In this case, the attempt was made to further develop the capital Astana into a regional financial center, in particular by establishing a special economic zone that is separate from the national law. Instead, the laws of England and Wales govern this enclave and the case law is transferred to English judges. Whether this is a step in the right direction, remains to be seen.

4. The Kazakh Enterprise Code

The main provisions on market regulation are specified in the *Enterprise Code* dated October 29, 2015 that contains general provisions on *business statutes, competition, antitrust* and *subsidy law*, among others. General rules on business regulation had already been reformed fundamentally the previous year in the *Law on Permits and Notification* dated May 16, 2014. However, the DBR 2018 shows a continuing need for reform as Kazakhstan only scores in the midfield in terms of the procedure for setting up businesses and acquiring a building permit. Mention should also be made of the *Law on Mineral Resources and Use of Mineral Resources* dated June 24, 2010 that was fundamentally revised on July 11, 2017. This law contains relevant provisions on the exploration and exploitation of domestic raw materials. Liberal tax legislation and the residency permits are further benefits for foreign investors.

5. The quality of Kazakh courts

The quality of the courts remains one of the construction sites of reform. Despite considerable progress, there are still short-comings. Reform of the judiciary with the aim of strengthening the independence of judges and the introduction of administrative courts are a high priority. In this context, it needs to be pointed out that judicial salaries have increased noticeably in recent times. Thus, an entry-level judge earns approx. USD 500 a month, which makes this profession comparatively attractive. Unlike many other countries, there is no Constitutional Court in Kazakhstan, there is the *Constitutional Council*. Nevertheless, the Council has the power to declare laws void for unconstitutionality.

In addition, foreign investors still have the option of evading the state courts by choosing arbitration tribunals. The relevant standards can be found in the *Law on Arbitration* of April 8, 2016. Arbitral awards must be enforced in Kazakhstan since the 1958 *New York Convention on the Recognition* and *Enforcement of International Arbitral Awards* has been in force there since 1996.

6. Foreign trade: membership in WTO and EEU

In terms of foreign trade, it is worth mentioning that Kazakhstan was admitted to the *WTO (World Trade Organization)* on November 30, 2015. At the same time, it is a member of the *Eurasian Economic Union (EEU)* — dominated by Russia and launched on January 1, 2015. The latter includes Russia, Kazakhstan, Armenia, Belarus and Kyrgyzstan. The main purpose of the EEU is to create a customs union comparable to the EEC in its early phase. Structurally, however, the *Eurasian Union* has only limited competences compared with the *European Union*. The *UN Sales Convention* has not yet been accepted by Kazakhstan as binding. However, it may be selected in a choice of law clause.

7. The 100 Concrete Steps Program and the 2025 strategy

Kazakhstan is also progressing in the fight against corruption, although efforts need to be continued. In *Transparency International's* ranking, the 2017 results are the best so far. On the positive side, the adoption of new anti-corruption laws, the creation of public control mechanisms and improvements in public procurement law have to be mentioned.

Against this background, the most recent reform programs are visible. In May 2015, *The 100 Concrete Steps Program,* drawn up by the Kazakh Government, was adopted, placing a focus on fighting corruption. The most recent measure was the edict dated February 15, 2018 confirming the *Development Strategy* until 2025. Seven priority areas of improvement have been identified including digitization as well as the "continuing leading role of the state sector in implementing reforms".

Prof. Dr. Hans-Joachim Schramm
joachim.schramm@ostinstitut.de

Part 3

German Companies Help Shape Modern Kazakhstan

BASF in Central Asia

KEY INDUSTRIES
Agriculture
Construction
Automotive
Oil & Gas
Mining

KEY FIGURES
Approx. 120 employees
2 Construction chemical production sites
in Almaty and Astana

BASF in Central Asia
Presence

BASF Central Asia LLP

LLP BASF Central Asia headquarter is located in Almaty and is a regional center for the markets in Kazakhstan, Kyrgyzstan, Tajikistan, Turkmenistan and Uzbekistan. The company is actively working in Central Asia and celebrated its 25th anniversary in Kazakhstan and Uzbekistan in 2017. Over the past years, BASF Central Asia has earned a reputation of a strong partner and a reliable manufacturer of high-quality materials and solutions.

About BASF

At BASF, we create chemistry for a sustainable future. We combine economic success with environmental protection and social responsibility. The more than 115 000 employees in the BASF Group work on contributing to the success of our customers in nearly all sectors and almost every country in the world. Our portfolio is organized into five divisions: Chemicals, Performance Products, Functional Materials & Solutions, Agricultural Solutions, and Oil & Gas. In 2017, EUR 64.5 billion were generated in turnover. The corporation's shares are traded on the stock exchanges in Frankfurt (BAS), London (BFA) and Zurich (BAS). For further information, visit www.basf.com.

BASF Central Asia LLP
050016, Rayimbek ave., 211A
Almaty Kazakhstan

Contact:

Rashid Kabykayev
Manager corporate communications and government relations
LLP BASF Central Asia,
3A, Charles De Gaulle,
010000 Astana, Kazakhstan

📞 +7 7172 27 04 40-110,
🔊 +7 701 029 67 38,
✉ rashid.kabykayev@basf.com

BASF: proximity and local empowerment

Interview with Ms. Saule Baitzhaunova, Managing Director, BASF Central Asia LLP

CCP: BASF Central Asia maintains offices and production sites in several countries and locations in Central Asia. That means you deal with different Asian cultures within your organization; the management challenge seems quite significant. Leadership principles and styles will vary when you compare German headquarters to Kazakhstan and other Central Asian states. Which principles and style do you apply at BASF in Kazakhstan?

SB: I do not perceive the diversity of cultures in our region as a difficult task. On the contrary, this is a unique opportunity to develop your management skills by contacting and working with different people from various cultures and areas. Of course, we adhere to the general BASF leadership principles and respect the customs and local traditions of an emerging market.

CCP: What does your management team look like at the site in Kazakhstan? Is it more local or an international team including German participation?

SB: We understand the cultural traditions of the region, importance of proximity and local empowerment. Hence, BASF places emphasis on developing colleagues and talents locally. Our management team consists of Kazakh, Uzbek, Turkmen and Ukrainian colleagues.

CCP: If the members of the board have different cultural backgrounds, do expectations vary on management style and problem solving at BASF Kazakhstan?

SB: Diversity is actually advantageous. It allows us to try out new techniques and view different opinions in decision-making.

CCP: How do you go about dealing with criticism regarding leadership style in general within the management board and with the staff?

SB: In line with our BASF strategy, we create space for performance and personal development for all our employees. It is possible to develop such an environment due to the existing corporate feedback culture and the feedback on a project. The "Tell me" project in our region allows any employee to give open and honest feedback to his or her manager or co-worker.

CCP: How many people work at BASF Central Asia today, especially in Kazakhstan, and how does this compare to the number of employees when BASF first started in Kazakhstan?

SB: Currently, we employ more than 120 people in BASF CA and we have offices in all the major cities in the region. It may not seem a high number, yet the chemical industry is unique in that by creating one job in our industry, a few additional positions in other fields result.

CCP: Your local employees need to understand the German technologies established in Kazakhstan and products you make here. They must be able to handle the German systems. How do you find employees with the necessary professional qualification?

SB: Our company places emphasis on qualifying the best local employees available in the region to form the best team. We train and develop them locally and in cross-country projects. In addition, colleagues from headquarters come here or we send our colleagues to headquarters depending on the complexity of a technology or product.

CCP: Are you planning to further expand the workforce?

SB: Currently, we are well equipped in the region with our organizational structure. It all depends on market conditions, but if a need for additional workforce arises, we may do that. As I mentioned before, by us creating one job in our industry, two or more positions in other industries result.

CCP: There are quite a number of foreign companies in Kazakhstan as well as in the neighboring countries, who may be attractive for local people. How do you motivate your Kazakh employees to stay with BASF, especially in Astana, Almaty and Atyrau?

SB: At BASF, we form the best teams. We attract the right people and create conditions for their effective professional and personal development. We create a working environment that inspires and unites the teams. We also instill a comprehensive leadership culture based on mutual trust, respect and commitment to maximum efficiency.

CCP: How you deal with employees is one aspect of management and how you interact with clients is another. What is special about client interaction in Kazakhstan compared to client relationship management in Germany?

SB: I would say proximity and the partnership approach. We treat our clients as close partners and do our best to contribute to their future success. As I mentioned, we work in the emerging market. Thus, being agile and able to react immediately to the needs of our customers is key.

CCP: At the sites in Kazakhstan, do you manufacture for the local market or do you also export to other Asian countries?

SB: We have two manufacturing sites in Almaty and Astana for construction chemicals that produce for the construction sector in the region. Mainly, we produce for local needs, yet we do export some to neighbouring countries.

CCP: You have gained extensive experience in the area of German-Central-Asian-Kazakh collaboration. What advice would you give to German managers or company owners thinking about setting up a subsidiary in Kazakhstan? Your advice could help them avoid mistakes and enable them to be successful from the start.

SB: Kazakhstan is a very attractive and promising market for investors where local government constantly works on improving the business climate. As a suggestion, I would first say market intelligence, preliminary comprehensive work on facts and figures. Then, of course, understanding the local mentality and cultural specifics. Lastly, thinking out of the box and being able to apply the German approach with Asian flexibility.

CCP: Ms. Baitzhaunova, we thank you very much for this interesting discussion. We are certain that your experience and insights will be useful for future German investors and executives.

BASF Central Asia LLP
050016, Rayimbek ave., 211A
Almaty Kazakhstan

Contact:

Rashid Kabykayev
Manager corporate communications and government relations
LLP BASF Central Asia,
3A, Charles De Gaulle,
010000 Astana, Kazakhstan

📞 +7 7172 27 04 40-110,
📶 +7 701 029 67 38,
✉ rashid.kabykayev@basf.com

Green Energy 3000 Group plans a 63 MWp solar power plant in southern Kazakhstan

The Green Energy 3000 Group has been planning a solar park with a rated solar capacity of 63 MWp in Chulakkurgan in southern Kazakhstan since 2016. The projected annual yield of the solar power plant of approx. 111 million kWh/year is so high that it can theoretically cover the electricity needs for a population of 21 625 in Kazakhstan. According to the 2018 edition of the CIA World Factbook, average electricity consumption there was 5 133 kWh/person in 2017.

The solar park will involve an area of approx. 148 acres. An additional transformer station with an output voltage of 110 000 volts will be erected directly at the solar park. It will serve to transmit the huge amount of electricity into the public KEGOC network. Plant construction will start in the fourth quarter of 2018. The total construction period will take 12 months.

"Kazakhstan is a very attractive country to target investments in the field of renewable energy," emphasized Andreas Renker, Managing Director of Green Energy 3000 Holding GmbH based in Leipzig. "Accession to the WTO in 2015, political stability, clear and investment-promoting structures, legal regulations in the area of encouraging green energy as well as ideal climate and weather conditions for wind and solar power plants are reasons enough for us to become involved in this country," explained Mr. Renker.

Green Energy 3000 took initial steps in the Central Asian country at the beginning of 2016. They now have a branch in Almaty and several local special-purpose vehicles to carry out projects in the field of renewable energy. In addition, shares in a construction company that possesses the know-how and approvals to perform the project construction were acquired. Green Energy 3000 plans to participate in the tender process for further environmentally friendly energy projects in Kazakhstan in the autumn of 2018.

The group is an experienced multinational project developer and general contractor in the renewable energy sector. Since 2004, Green Energy 3000 has gathered extensive know-how from site acquisition and project planning to international component purchasing, financing and the installation of solar and wind power plants. In addition, they offer international technical and commercial management (O&M) for the finished power plants.

As a new business area, Green Energy 3000 has been active in the energy storage field since 2017 thus allowing manufacturing companies to reduce their electricity costs. The group also actively contributes to enabling the further expansion of Renewable Energy chances through load peak management and relief to the grid involved. A total of 50 employees in Germany, France and Kazakhstan contribute to the success of the company.

Green Energy 3000 GmbH
Torgauer Strasse 231
DE-04347 Leipzig, Germany
📞 +49 (0)341 35 56 04 0
✉ info@ge3000.de
🌐 www.ge3000.de

TOO Green Energy 3000 Kazakhstan
Mukanov Street, 113
Business Center "Rich"
050026 Almaty
Republic of Kazakhstan

Kazakhstan offers extremely attractive conditions for Renewable Energy

Interview with
Mr. Andreas Renker, Dipl. Ing.,
Managing Director Green Energy
3000 Holding GmbH, Leipzig

CCP: Mr. Renker, your company is named Green Energy 3000. For what does 3000 stand?

AR: The number 3000, in combination with the reference to green energy, expresses the idea of sustainability in all its facets. In this sense, the 3000 stands for the future and inexhaustible renewable power generation. These are values our company has stood for since it was founded.

CCP: You have been working in the very important sector of Renewable Energy in Kazakhstan since 2016. Is the country already producing part of its national energy in this sector or only from fossil raw materials, such as Karaganda hard coal?

AR: Kazakhstan is making enormous efforts to cover a large part of its electricity requirements from Renewable Energy sources in the medium term. There is a very great potential here, which, however, is currently hardly exploited. However, this will change dramatically in the coming years.

CCP: Which criteria led your company to choose Kazakhstan as its investment site?

AR: Kazakhstan offers extremely attractive conditions for Renewable Energy. The basis is the climate conditions, characterized by attractive windy regions and, especially in the south, by strong solar irradiation. In the southern part of the country, photovoltaic systems generate completely different amounts of electricity per installed kWp output/ year than, for example, in Germany. The structures and legal regulations in the area of promoting Renewable Energy encourage investments on this basis. Last but not least, accession to the WTO in 2015 and quite a high degree of political stability added to this decision.

CCP: In which way is your company present in Kazakhstan: through a representative office or dealers, or do you already produce there?

AR: We have a representative office that works hand in hand with our project managers at our head office in Leipzig and acts on our behalf. This allows us to closely link our international and interdisciplinary team at our headquarters with our local project management and expertise.

CCP: What type of Renewable Energy do you plan to develop more strongly in Kazakhstan?

AR: We are currently focusing on photovoltaics and wind power. The construction of our 63 MWp photovoltaic plant in Chulakkurgan will begin still in 2018. We are also preparing additional projects, including wind farms, in concrete terms. Other areas, such as biogas, also offer interesting opportunities in the medium term.

CCP: Kazakhstan has long winters with much snow and many blizzards. What will become of your solar systems during this season?

AR: Chulakkurgan lies in a steppe region and is characterized by a continental climate. Precipitation that has a negative effect on the yield of our plant is relatively rare in this region. In addition, due to its southern location, irradiation values are high throughout the year, even in winter, although the irradiation is, of course, significantly lower than in the summer. This seasonal cycle exists almost everywhere.

CCP: Kazakhstan has infinitely large steppe areas as well as mountains up to 23,000 feet high. Have you considered building wind farms?

AR: Wind farms are also among our investment projects in Kazakhstan. There are many attractive windy regions with high average air speeds, for example in the north of the country.

CCP: The climate is associated with unforeseeable fluctuations and even storms that cause failures and thus losses in electricity production from the sun and/or wind. Would it not be safer to develop Renewable Energy from the bio-waste of Kazakh agriculture?

AR: This would be a good supplement to the energy sources previously described since biomass is less weather-dependent. The energy transition requires utilizing various energy sources.

CCP: Green Energy 3000 is certainly not alone in the Kazakh market. Canadians and Americans are probably also active in your field. What distinguishes your plants from theirs?

AR: Investors from diverse countries are involved in Kazakhstan, last but not least in the newly created tenders. Our aim is to establish ourselves in this market with German engineering skills and to achieve the best possible quality in the components used. This enables us to ensure that the systems run for the required duration without restrictions and at the same time use state-of-the-art technology.

CCP: Which goals have you set for the development of your company in Kazakhstan over the next five years and within the framework of the nation's development program until 2050?

AR: We would like to further establish ourselves in the Kazakh market by completing several projects and being successful within the framework of the newly created tender model. As a perspective, we would, of course, be satisfied by becoming a major contributor to the energy transition in Kazakhstan and to contribute as a key player to harnessing the country's great potential in the field of renewable energy.

CCP: Do you work with Kazakh power experts?

AR: A close cooperation with local and regional experts is essential for any green energy assignment. In Kazakhstan, cooperating with Kazakh experts is important, for example within the scope of the necessary expertise and for obtaining a building permit. We are pleased to be able to expand our regional expertise even further.

CCP: In which languages do you operate in Kazakhstan?

AR: In our international team you can hear not only German and French but also Kazakh, Russian and English, depending on the situation.

CCP: How would you describe the cooperation with the state administration in Kazakhstan during the start-up period of your company?

AR: We found a mild business climate and were able to address our issues every time. We do not have any reason to complain.

CCP: What experience in German-Kazakh cooperation would you like to pass on to German executives or company owners who come to Kazakhstan after you?

AR: In addition to the otherwise coherent business model for market entry, knowledge of local and regional specifics is a key success factor. Anyone who can move confidently both linguistically and culturally on site has a better chance of success.

CCP: Thank you very much, dear Mr. Renker, for your interesting statements. They will certainly be helpful for future German investors in Kazakhstan.

Green Energy 3000 GmbH
Torgauer Strasse 231
DE-04347 Leipzig, Germany
📞 +49 (0)341 35 56 04 0
✉ info@ge3000.de
🌐 www.ge3000.de

TOO Green Energy 3000 Kazakhstan
Mukanov Street, 113
Business Center "Rich"
050026 Almaty
Republic of Kazakhstan

Europe-Asia Bridge:

LORENZ Handels GmbH, Neuhof, Germany
and
Managing Company Shanyrak Ltd.,
Astana, Kasakhstan

General Manager:
Alexander Lorenz
📞 +7 (7172) 55 28 54
📶 +7 701 888 87 71
✉ a.lorenz@shanyrak-group.kz
🌐 www.shanyrak-group.kz

The Shanyrak Group

- **Capital Projects Ltd.**
  Producers of compound feed and chicken meat products, 600 jobs
- **Agrointerptiza GmbH**
  Producers of commercial eggs, 230 jobs
- **Poultry farmo perated under the name K. Marx GmbH**
  Producer of eggs for commercial purposes, 220 jobs
- **Geflügelfarm (poultry farm) Tselinogradskaja GmbH**
  Producer of eggs for commercial purposes, 85 jobs
- **Plemptizetorg GmbH**
  Commercial poultry breeding for egg production, 60 jobs
- **Energia-Kapital GmbH**
  Producers of baked goods
- **JSC Akmola – Feniks AG, Akmola-Feniks Plus**
  TOO Shanyrak Agro: Plant production, producers of animal feed, 93 900 acres, 335 jobs
- **Eco Pack Astana GmbH**
  Producers of egg packaging, 21 jobs
- **Bio-Katu Ltd.**
  Producers of organic fertilizers

LORENZ Handels GmbH, Neuhof, Germany, and Managing Company Shanyrak Ltd., Astana, Kazakhstan

LORENZ Handels GmbH is a bridge between Europe and Asia in Neuhof, Germany, as it is the purchasing organization for the Managing Company Shanyrak Ltd. in Kazakhstan.

Alexander Lorenz equips his companies in Kazakhstan with the most modern machines from Europe: Germany, Belgium, The Netherlands and Switzerland.

The Managing Company Shanyrak Ltd. is headquartered in the Kazakh capital of Astana and runs a group of eleven agricultural companies based in various parts of western Kazakhstan — from Kokshetau in the Aqmola Region in the north through Karaganda to Almaty in the south. It employs 1 800 people and is constantly growing.

On the basis of 93 900 acres of agricultural land, the group produces 40,000 tons of animal feed per year for five farms and operates a bread factory. They also make their own egg packaging from waste paper collected in the cities.

The Managing Company Shanyrak Ltd. produced 360 million eggs in 2017 for export to Russia, Afghanistan, Tajikistan and is expanding its exports to Iran. In addition, the group produces 20 000 tons of chicken poultry products per year and daily supplies 500 stores in Astana and the surrounding area with chicken poultry products.

The Managing Company Shanyrak Ltd. aims to become a completely independent value chain.

Managing Company Shanyrak GmbH
Alexander Lorenz
General Manager
Akmola Region, Tselinograd Bezirk,
Dorf Akmol, Str. Gagarina 14
021800, Republik Kasachstan
📞 +7 772 55 28 54
📶 +7 701 886 87 71
✉ a.lorenz@shanyrak-group.kz
🌐 www.shanyrak-group.kz

Success in Kazakhstan.
The Lorenz strategy: Start small, stay active and work right. Based on initial success, build trust and then grow.

Interview with Mr. Alexander Lorenz, General Manager of the Managing Company Shanyrak Ltd., Astana

CCP: *Mr. Lorenz, before we start — thank you for your willingness to do this interview because as the managing director of a network of approx. eleven subsidiary companies your daily schedule is full of appointments. May the readers of this book learn something about your background? Your surname is German and your first name is Russian. When did your great-great-grandparents emigrate to Kazakhstan and why did they do so?*

AL: My ancestors are from Baunatal near Kassel. They were peasants and followed the call of Empress Catherine II in 1763 to settle on the Volga, in the autonomous region promised to them. They grew wheat and ran a farm. In the Stalin era before the Second World War, they were deported further east in the Soviet Union, to Kazakhstan. They had to work on a co-operative-run farm. My father was six years old at the time.

CCP: So you were born in Kazakhstan, the son of parents who were kolkhoz (co-operative-run type) farmers and grew up in the Karaganda Region where you also went to school.

AL: Yes, indeed.

CCP: *Where did you receive your vocational training and what did you study?*

AL: I first completed training in Astana (then Zelinograd), then studied at the University of Arkalyk and later at the East Kazakhstan University in Ust-Kaminogorsk. I studied technology, commerce and economics.

CCP: *Today, you have untold management knowledge and skills. How did your career go?*

AL: After completing my training, I worked for ten years at various companies in Arkalyk, then thirteen years as a deputy director in Eastern Kazakhstan. In Arkalyk, I married Tatjana in 1973 and then our two children were born. My daughter, Viktoria, was born in the year 1974 and my son, Alexej, in 1978. Meanwhile, my parents had gone back to Germany and I followed them with my family in 1996. First, I studied German intensively and then I founded my first company in Neuhof. I sold German machinery for poultry farms and chicken feed to Russia and Kazakhstan.

CCP: *Yes, this Neuhof company is managed by your wife today, and you have founded numerous other companies in Kazakhstan. That seems easy. What would you recommend a German medium-sized entrepreneur do to be as successful as you in Kazakhstan?*

AL: There is enough work to do in Kazakhstan. You just have to know what you want, come, look around and make contacts, first with the city council. There are many ways to obtain grants and help of every kind. Demand for investors in Kazakhstan is high. However, you also have to be patient and be very active yourself.

CCP: *In your opinion, is agriculture the area where German SMEs have the greatest chance of contributing to modernization?*

AL: Yes, absolutely. Assistance will certainly be provided: you just have to submit the relevant applications to the state. The German-Kazakh organization *Wiedergeburt (Rebirth)* also offers help.

CCP: *That sounds very promising. Could you name some areas of activity, where the know-how of the German middle class in Kazakhstan is very much in demand and necessary?*

AL: Germans are valued everywhere in Kazakhstan. We owe this positive image to the good work of our ancestors. Good, honest and trustworthy — these are the standards attributed to Germans and that you expect. This image of the Germans was created already on the collective farm through good work. They achieved a lot.

CCP: *That's true. And you have done a lot too. You need many different specialists for your various companies: for operating modern monitor-controlled agricultural machines and processing plants from Germany, Switzerland and Belgium; for scientifically justified animal feed production; for effective egg and meat production; 24-hour logistics; and more. Where do you find these numerous specialists?*

AL: We invite experts from different countries: from Germany, The Netherlands and other European countries to our trainings. We offer theoretical training combined with practical applications. This is how we obtain good specialists.

CCP: *Living and working in the Kazakh countryside is probably not as comfortable as living in Astana. How do you motivate your employees to work and stay in your companies?*

AL: In the countryside, there was no work at first — no matter where. Then, for example, we built the modern chicken poultry farm with the highest pay level in Akmola in the Akmola Region. In addition, our employees receive free work clothes, company benefits in the workplace, such as washing, shower, changing and dining rooms, free meals, as well as social insurance. Now people are coming back from the city to the village and want to work with us.

CCP: *What recommendations do you give a German company manager for dealing with Kazakh personnel so that cooperation is successful?*

AL: Be friendly, honest and understanding but not pretentious. Of course you should speak the language of the staff.

CCP: *If there are issues in the production process, be it energy, water, building or other hiccups, are there local partners who can help?*

AL: The local people, in the city or area administration like helping. You just have to explain your issue and look for solutions together with them.

CCP: *There currently is no German bank in Kazakhstan. German companies have to cooperate with Kazakh banks locally. You have a lot of experience in this field. Can you help a German medium-sized entrepreneur who does not obtain a loan in Germany to receive financing for company growth in Kazakhstan?*

AL: It depends on the project. Every bank needs collateral, for example, buildings or the like. You do not have to want everything in the beginning, yet start small, be modest and hardworking, show what you can do, build trust with your first successes and then grow naturally step by step. For example, in garbage processing, start with one piece of equipment, show the positive effects to the people at the bank and then you will definitely get further support.

CCP: *You are now 65 years old, the head of a very successful group of* companies, have received numerous state awards and still have future goals. What do you still wish to accomplish?

AL: First, I want to expand the existing chicken poultry farms to include fertilizer production and meat processing. Furthermore, we plan to build a factory to process eggs into egg powder that meets the world-wide standards, the needs of Kazakhstan and for export.

CCP: *These are big plans, Mr. Lorenz. In any case, we wish you continued success in your present and future endeavors.*

Managing Company Shanyrak GmbH
Alexander Lorenz
General Manager
Akmola Region, Tselinograd Bezirk,
Dorf Akmol, Str. Gagarina 14
021800, Republik Kasachstan
☎ +7 772 55 28 54
🕾 +7 701 886 87 71
✉ a.lorenz@shanyrak-group.kz
🌐 www.shanyrak-group.kz

Amazonen-Werke
H. Dreyer GmbH & Co.KG

Amazonen-Werke, headquartered in Hasbergen-Gaste, not far from Osnabrück in northern Germany, manufactures agricultural and municipal machinery. The company, which is owned and managed by the Dreyer family, employs approx. 1,850 people at seven different production sites in Germany, France, Russia and Hungary.

The production range includes soil tillage machines, seed drills, fertilizer spreaders and crop protection sprayers. Based on these core competencies, Amazone is now the specialist for intelligent crop production in agriculture. Amazone also produces machinery for park and lawn maintenance as well as winter road gritting. Amazone has an excellent reputation among its customers thanks to its superior quality and innovative products.

In 2017, Amazone sold machinery worth approx. EUR 457 million. Over the course of its more than 135-year history, Amazone has grown into a globally operating systems provider, with approx. 80 percent of its production now sold in over 70 countries.

To respond to this trend and to demonstrate the required presence in the target markets in Asia, the management decided to establish a subsidiary called Amazone TOO in Kazakhstan's capital, Astana, in 2010. This step enabled the quality required locally in the field of sales consulting and the development of after sales service. With close to 50 million acres of arable land, Kazakhstan is an important market for Amazonen-Werke. In order to meet the requirements of our customers, we have opened other sites in the agricultural area in the north, in Kostanay and Kokshetau, in addition to headquarters in Astana.

An extensive stock of spare parts has also been built up in Kokshetau to allow us to optimally look after the machinery at any time of the season. A large proportion of the Kazakh employees are trained annually at the main plant in Germany. This is absolutely essential, as the most advanced and innovative machinery from Amazone is in operation in the fields of Kazakhstan.

Amazone TOO in Astana is also actively involved in the new and further development of Amazone machinery. For example, in cooperation with German and Kazakh research institutes, machinery is developed and tested to meet the specific demands in northern Kazakhstan. This is supported by the German Federal Ministry of Education and Research in the form of the "ReKKS" project.

AMAZONE TOO
Republic of Kazakhstan,
Astana 010000, Rayon Saryarka
Saifullina-Straße 3, Haus 3, Büro 1
📞 +7 705 29 51 88 6,
📶 +49 151 17 11 77 01
✉ Dr.Tobias.Meinel@amazone.de

ТОО «АМАЗОНЕ»
Республика Казахстан,
010000, город Астана, район Сарыарка
ул. Сейфуллина д. 3,НП-1
📞 +7 717 23 47 9 49, +7 701 52 40 914
✉ Dr.Tobias.Meinel@amazone.de
   Oxana.Privalenko@amazone.kz

AMAZONEN-WERKE H. Dreyer GmbH & Co. KG
Am Amazonenwerk 9-13
D-49205 Hasbergen, Germany
📞 +49 (0)5405 501-0
✉ amazone@amazone.de
🌐 www.amazone.de

Amazone: Agronomic and technical solutions for sustainable crop production in the Eurasian Steppe

Interview with Dr. rer. nat.
Tobias Meinel, General Director of
TOO Amazone, Astana, Kazakhstan

CCP: Dr. Meinel, Amazone is now a specialist in the world market for intelligent crop production in agriculture and it was with this profile that your company started selling state-of-the-art agricultural technology in 2010. You have been managing Sales Consulting and After Sales Service for eight years now. How many employees do you have?

TM: There are 12 Kazakh employees at our branch here in Astana, who are qualified to optimally look after our machinery on site as a result of our training.

CCP: We are interested in Amazone's contribution to the modernization of agriculture in Kazakhstan. In order to understand this, could you please describe the state of the agricultural technology that you found here in the initial year 2010?

TM: To put it simply, we often found agricultural technology on a par with that from 1975. This means that the farmers were sowing seeds with out-dated seed drills and were not using fertilizer or crop protection products.

CCP: Shouldn't we assume that young Kazakh agronomists from the local universities have long been bringing fresh ideas into their country's agriculture?

TM: Just like everywhere else in the world, fresh ideas in Kazakhstan tend to come from the university graduates in particular. The young people here are highly motivated and willing to work. The younger generation wants progress, is eager to learn and certainly often presents some teaching staff with a real challenge. The young academics want to study state-of-the-art production methods and take advantage of agricultural progress. It is important that these young agronomists are offered prospects in local agriculture and not just in the capital Astana.

CCP: This means that you also have to offer advanced training with the sale of state-of-the-art Amazone agricultural technology. You look after an agricultural area in the north and northwest with a scope of 700 x 1 000 km. How many people in this area have you instructed in how to operate your state-of-the-art machinery over the course of eight years?

TM: Certainly over 700. These are two of our assets: training – both theoretical and practical on the machinery itself on the farm as well as in use on the field – and 24-hour service availability. To implement and support this service, we maintain a very extensive stock of spare parts in Kokshetau. Within 24 hours we can deliver spare parts to the remotest village in Kazakhstan. If a necessary spare part is ever not in stock, we can supply it from Germany within 3 days.

CCP: Training requires language. Do you speak perfect Russian?

TM: Yes, I studied in Barnaul, in Russia. Among other things, speaking Russian helps me with my job in Kazakhstan.

CCP: Could you describe in a little more detail the cutting-edge technology that you introduce into Kazakh agriculture here?

TM: I would be happy to. It is basically agronomic and technical solutions for sustainable crop production in the Eurasian Steppe, in other words, resource-saving agriculture and the introduction of innovative climate-adapted agricultural technology. One part of this is large-area sowing technology. A field is approx. 2 x 2 kilometres in size! Our Amazone seed drill is 15 m wide, and can sow and spread fertilizer at the same time. Our crop protection sprayers are satellite-controlled. The tractor is controlled so that no area remains untreated and the tractor operator can closely monitor his work progress on a screen.

CCP: Crop protection products: these are presumably products used to protect against pest infestations, so-called pesticides, is that right?

TM: Yes, partly. Particularly important is the tailored application of herbicides that control the competing weeds.

CCP: On huge areas of land, this certainly incurs immense costs, and it can also be ecologically harmful. Does Amazone have an agronomic technical solution for this?

TM: Yes, this solution is called UX *AmaSpot*. Amazone is the only company in the world that manufactures such a machine. The booms of the machine are fitted with sensors that selectively detect weedsgrowing and can therefore destroy them selectively, instead of spraying the whole field unnecessarily with the chemical weed killer. So at the same time, the soil and crops are spared and immense cost savings are achieved.

CCP: That sounds great, Dr. Meinel, and enables Kazakh agriculture to achieve high yields. Yet, but can the farms afford to buy all this machinery?

TM: With this question you've touched a sore spot. Farmers are keen to buy this machinery, but they run into a problem that should be solved at a political level beforehand. In Kazakhstan, loans are very expensive. The German banks only grant loans with a term of six months because Hermes currently only provides insurance for six months. As in other countries, the farmer needs a loan period of at least three years, so that he can finance the investment with the proceeds from three harvests.

CCP: We can only hope, Dr. Meinel, that this problem is sufficiently well known and that the solution is already being worked on. What are Amazone's goals for the future?

TM: Our goals are to continue to provide excellent crop production advice, sell more of our machinery, promote sustainability without destroying the soil in Kazakhstan, provide more in-depth sales advice, maintain and intensify the day and night services while achieving and maintaining extensive customer satisfaction.

CCP: We wish you every success in achieving them. But before we say goodbye, I have one more question about the future:

What message would you like to give to future German executives who come to Kazakhstan?

TM: Knowing the native languages and traditions is an advantage, because it creates the necessary personal relationship of trust, which is essential for good cooperation. You also need a lot of patience, because the republic is still young and development in the countryside is sometimes not as fast as it is in the city. However, I can only recommend coming to Kazakhstan – it is a great pleasure to learn, work and live alongside the people here. This is why I have been here for eight years.

CCP: Many thanks for such an interesting discussion.

Dr. rer. nat. Tobias Meinel
✉ Dr.Tobias.Meinel@amazone.de

Plant for high-performance pipe insulation Isoplus Central Asia LLP

The pipe insulation plant Isoplus Central Asia LLP is the Kazakh subsidiary of the Isoplus group of companies in Europe. Isoplus manufactures pre-insulated pipe systems for district heating and all types of industrial purposes.

The president of our country, Nursultan Nazarbayev, opened the plant in 2014 when the entire production technology was taken over from the parent company, Isoplus Central Asia LLP. This allowed German quality in the manufacture of pre-insulated pipes and fittings to be established in Kazakhstan. By using high-quality materials and new technologies, we achieved the best performance in such important parameters as:

- Thermal conductivity,
- Insulation quality,
- Quality of the insulation at the pipe joint,
- Service life of pre-insulated heating networks,
- Optimized pipelines.

Isoplus Central Asia is the first producer in the CIS countries (Commonwealth of Independent States) that makes and uses a heat-insulating material on the basis of a cyclopentane where the coefficient of thermal conductivity is 0.0275 W/(m*K).

Isoplus uses a dual-component system (polyol and isocyanate) from BASF and hydrocarbon cyclopentane as a foaming agent. In the process of exothermic and chemical reactions, a high-quality hard insulation material is produced with an improved thermal conductivity of 0.0275 W/(m*K), EN 253. This results in reducing heating loss in the heat supply networks by approx. 30 percent compared to the traditional insulation material used based on CO_2 and freon.

Isoplus Central Asia is the leading manufacturer of pipe insulation in Kazakhstan. Some company facts are:

- Number of employees: 150.
- Production capacity 2017: DN1 000-100 km/year, DN500 1 km/day.
- Market coverage: 60 percent.
- Value own warehouse of finished products: EUR 2 million.
- Transportation logistics to all14 regions by road and rail delivery (terms: DDP).
- Distance of the furthest delivery: 2 895 km (Aktau).
- Sales portfolio: 200 km of pipe products in various diameters as well as approx. 10 000 different formed products.

Isoplus Central Asia is the only manufacturer of pre-insulated pipes that provides services for the insulation of pipe joints (filling couplings with polyurethane foam) with its own mobile equipment on the basis of the VW Crafter.

For the high-quality insulation of pipe junctions in main heating networks, our specially trained serviceman is ready to go to the construction site to fill and insulate the cavities of couplings using the mobile equipment.

Isoplus Central Asia LLP

4 Republic Avenue
590-591Qaraghandy, Kazakhstan
- +7 (7212) 78 24 84,
  +7 (7212) 78 88 41,
  +7 (701) 801-85-17
- kim.a@tooksm.kz
- tooksm.kz

We can only succeed once we have understood the local mentality and been patient enough

Interview with
Mr. Leonard Stein, General Manager,
Isoplus Central Asia LLP

CCP: Welcome to this interview, Mr. Stein, and thank you for your willingness to share some of Isoplus' experiences in Kazakhstan with the readers of this book. With a manufacturing plant for insulated tube systems, your company has been successfully operating in Kazakhstan since 2014. This is certainly displayed in the increasing employee figures. You began with just a few employees. How many people currently work for Isoplus in Karaganda?

LS: Since production start in Kazakhstan in 2014, the number of employees has more than tripled. Isoplus employs 150 people today and the trend is rising.

CCP: Several languages are common in Kazakhstan. Which ones are used in your company?

LS: Our staff is multilingual. However, we do not have a corporate language. It has turned out that approx. 20 percent of the workforce speaks German very well and can communicate with German co-workers without any problems. English is also very important, as we want to do our procurement worldwide and export products.

CCP: Do you also have German employees?

LS: Since we have already achieved a certain level of production, we can do without the constant presence of our German colleagues. As previously mentioned, approx. 20 percent of our employees are German-speaking.

CCP: The direct German style in communicating often causes friction in an Asian environment where the style is generally indirect. Is this compensated by the use of English?

LS: In Kazakhstan, as in the other Central Asian countries, our directness is now accepted, as our partners have very little time for discussion.

CCP: As indicated previously, Kazakhstan is a nation of great ethnic and religious diversity. How do you deal with this reality in recruitment?

LS: Neither of these factors play any role. We hire people who can demonstrate the required special know-how and who are motivated enough.

CCP: While the qualification of a candidate for employment in your factory is important, cultural diversity implies different leadership ideas and how people interact in the work place. Is this a source of conflict?

LS: Not really. To repeat it: technical know-how is the priority here.

CCP: Which leadership style is practiced at your plant in Karaganda, for example: German, Isoplus in-house or Kazakh?

LS: It is a mix of the German and Kazakh styles.

CCP: So you are successful with this style. How would you describe its basic features?

LS: Acceptance, a certain freedom in making decisions and almost invisible control.

CCP: How is the management team put together, e.g., Kazakh, Kazakh-German or international?

LS: Only Kazakh.

CCP: Was it like that from the beginning or is the current state the result of years of experience since the plant opened in 2014? I think our readers could learn a lot from you in this respect.

LS: It has been the result of years of experience.

CCP: Next, let's move on to work organization. Geographers say the climate in Kazakhstan is continental, so that it can become very hot in the summer and freezing cold in the winter. Does that affect the work scheduling and work processes in general?

LS: The weather has a huge impact on the structure and organization, starting with our customers since our business is climate-related and therefore seasonal. In the wintertime, we always reckon with not being able to obtain or deliver any goods due to the frosty temperatures or snow. Last winter, for example, the roads were closed 36 times in total.

CCP: Of course, that's quite significant. What about your production and the labor market in Kazakhstan? Can you easily find the skilled workers you need on site?

LS: This point cannot be generalized since it depends on the job profile.

There are special positions where we require months before we can hire a specialist. It is really very difficult, especially for a manufacturing firm to find someone with the right qualifications.

CCP: The production of your insulated tube systems certainly is short of important know-how that is only accessible in the German parent company. How do you make it available to the executives and employees in Qaraghandy?

LS: Almost all of our employees are trained in Germany, or by German colleagues on site in Karaganda. Training is vital and we do not want to save on that.

CCP: Do you conduct regular qualification courses, also for newcomers?

LS: Certainly, at the moment, we have more than ten employees with a second university degree and even two with a doctorate. Continuing education courses take place constantly.

CCP: Numerous foreign companies are active in Kazakhstan. How do you motivate local staff to come and stay with Isoplus?

LS: We offer a good working atmosphere as well as excellent opportunities for training and further development. In addition, we pay above average.

CCP: Based on your many years of experience and success in Kazakhstan, what would you recommend to German medium-sized companies who want to become equally successful in launching their business in Kazakhstan in the near future?

LS: We will not be successful until we understand the local mentality and are patient enough.

CCP: Thank you, Mr. Stein, for this interview. You certainly provided us with some interesting insights into business in Kazakhstan for other German medium-sized companies as investors.

Isoplus Central Asia LLP

4 Republic Avenue
590-591Karaganda, Kazakhstan
📞 +7 (7212) 78 24 84,
   +7 (7212) 78 88 41.
   +7 (701) 801-85-77
✉ kim.a@tooksm.kz
🌐 tooksm.kz

Annexe

Bildquellen/Photo credits

All pictures by Cross-Culture Publishing, except
page 86 Managing Company Shanyrak,
page 87 Amazone-Werke H. Dreyer GmbH & Co. KG,
page 91 http://www.wikipedia.org/wiki/Караганда,
page 95 German-Kazakh University (dku.kz).

Kasachstan in Deutschland
Kazakhstan in Germany

Botschaft der Republik Kasachstan in Deutschland

Nordendstrasse 14-17 13156 Berlin
☎ +49 (0)30 47 00 71 11 ✉ info@botschaft-kaz.de
🌐 www.botschaft-kasachstan.de

Außenstelle der Botschaft Kasachstans in Bonn

Rathaustrasse 3, 53225 Bonn
☎ +49 (0)228 40 38 70
✉ konsulbonn@gmail.com

Generalkonsulat der Republik Kasachstan in Frankfurt am Main

Beethovenstrasse 17, 60325 Frankfurt am Main
☎ +49 (0)69 97 14 67 0
✉ info.kaz@genconsul.de

Konsulat der Republik Kasachstan in München

Redwitzstrasse 4, 81925 München
☎ +49 (0)89 90 90 10 601
✉ Konsul-muenchen@mfa.kz

Honorarkonsulat der Republik Kasachstan in Stuttgart

Rotenwaldstrasse 100, 70197 Stuttgart
☎ +49 (0)711 50 53 08 9 1
✉ honorarkonsulat.kasachstan@haller-logistics.com

Honorarkonsulat der Republik Kasachstan in Dresden

Loschwitzer Strasse 15, 01309 Dresden
☎ +49 (0)351 31 21 560
✉ honorarkonsulat@cac-chem.de

Honorarkonsulat der Republik Kasachstan in Hannover.

Anderter Strasse 99D, 30559 Hannover
☎ +49 (0)511 30 18 68 99
✉ konsul-hannover@t-online.de

Honorarkonsulat der Republik Kasachstan in Bremen

Karl-Ferdinand-Braun Strasse 8, 28359 Bremen
☎ +49 (0)421 20 20 614, 20 20 8
✉ ohb@ohb-system.de

Modernes Kasachstan

Deutschland in Kasachstan
Germany in Kazakhstan

Botschaft der Bundesrepublik Deutschland
Cosmonauts-Strasse 62, Astana 010000, Kasachstan
📞 +7 71 72 79 12 00 ✉ kasachstan.diplo.de

Konsularischer Amtsbezirk: Astana, Karaganda, Ostkasachstan (Öskemen), Pawlodar, Nordkasachstan (Petropawlowsk), Akmolinsk (Kokschetau), Kostanai.

Generalkonsulat der Bundesrepublik Deutschland
Ivanilova-Strasse 2, 050059 Almaty
📞 +7 72 72 62 83 41, +7 72 72 62 83 46
🌐 www.almaty-diplo.de

Konsularischer Amtsbezirk: Almaty, Gebiet Almaty (Taldykorgan), Shambyl (Taras), Südkasachstan (Schymkent), Kysylorda, Aktobe, Mangystau (Aktau), Atyrau, Westkasachstan (Uralsk).

Cross-Culture Publishing

Reihe Wirtschaft &Kultur
The Economy & Culture Series

Vol. 19   Vol. 20   Vol. 21   Vol. 22

Reihe City International
The City International Series

Cross-Culture Publishing, Dr. Susanne Mueller

Bettinastrasse 30, D-60325 Frankfurt/Main, Germany

📞 +49 (0)69 173 204 220

✉ mail@cc-publishing.com

www.cc-publishing.com